Introductory Pascal

B.J. Holmes B.Sc, M.Sc, MBCS, Cert.Ed.

Principal Lecturer in the School of Computing and Mathematical
Sciences, Oxford Brookes University, Headington, Oxford, OX3 0BP

DP Publications
Aldine Place
London W12 8AW
0181 740 2266

1993

Disclaimer

The programs presented in this book have been included for their instructional value. They have been computer-tested with considerable care and are not guaranteed for any particular purpose. The author does not offer any warranties or representations, nor does he accept any liabilities with respect to the programs.

A CIP catalogue record for this book is available from the British Library

First Edition 1993
Reprinted 1994, 1997

ISBN 1 85805 007 3

© 1993 B.J.Holmes

Typeset and illustrated by B.J.Holmes

Printed by The Guernsey Press Company Ltd, Braye Road, Vale, Guernsey, Channel Islands.

Contents

iv

Preface

Audience

This book is written for the beginner, and does not assume any prior knowledge of computer programming.

The text is intended to be used by people from very diverse backgrounds and disciplines who have the common aim of wanting to know the fundamentals of computer programming.

The examples used in the text and questions, with the exception of the final chapter, are deliberately chosen to be of a non-mathematical nature.

This book should prove useful to students who are required to study computer programming for the following examinations.

- GCSE in Computer Studies

- Advanced level GCE in Computer Studies

- City & Guilds 726 Information Technology Scheme

- IDPM Foundation Course F11

- NCC International Diploma in Computer Studies - Unit 2

Format

In *Introductory Pascal* the emphasis throughout the book is on the use of carefully chosen examples that highlight the features of the language being studied. Explanation about the language follows from, and is put into context with, the example programs.

The development of the language statements and the programs are taken in manageable steps, to enable the reader to build a firm foundation of knowledge. The type of programming examples used are simple enough to give the reader confidence at each stage of learning Pascal.

A section on programming questions is found at the end of each chapter. These questions serve to test the reader's understanding of the topics, and reinforce the material of the chapter. The reader is advised to complete the answers to the questions before progressing to the next chapter. The answers to all the questions are given towards the end of the book.

Language and computer requirements

Studying Pascal can be more effective and enjoyable if a computer is used for running both the demonstration programs and the reader's own answers to the programming questions.

The author has used Turbo Pascal version 5.0 from Borland International in the preparation of all the programs listed in this book.

All the programs have been developed and tested on an IBM PC compatible microcomputer using MSDOS.

Brief history

Pascal is a high-level computer language, invented by Niklaus Wirth, a computer scientist at the Institute of Informatics in Zurich. In 1971 he published his language, and named it after the seventeenth-century French mathematician and philosopher, Blaise Pascal (1623-1662), who invented a calculating machine. The language was slightly modified in a revised form in 1973.

Pascal may be regarded as the first language that many students use during their studies about computing. Indeed it is regarded by many examining boards as the de facto programming language.

Lecturers' Supplement

A disc containing all the demonstration programs and answers, is available free of charge, from DP Publications, to lecturers adopting the book as a course text.

BJH - Oxford May 1993

1.
Facts and figures

This introductory chapter contains information about data found in everyday life. It explores the different characteristics of data such as type, size and format, and illustrates how to represent the format of data using syntax diagrams. The method of declaring data in the Pascal language is also examined.

Contents

1.1 What is data?

The word data has found its way into everyday language, but what does it mean? The Concise Oxford Dictionary definition of data is "..1 known facts or things used as a basis for inference or reckoning. 2 quantities or characters operated on by a computer etc..". Put another way, data can be numbers and/ or groups of characters that represent facts. Consider the diagram of the road sign in figure 1.1, it represents a typical everyday example of data. The road sign contains two items of data, the name of the town Keswick, and a distance to Keswick of 15 miles. Hence a group of characters represent the name and a number represents the distance.

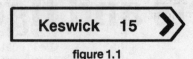

Keswick   15

figure 1.1

There are plenty of examples of data in everyday life. Figure 1.2 illustrates a typical menu in a cafe. The names of the items of food or drink are represented by groups of characters and the price of each item by a number.

Greasy Spoon Cafe

MENU

fruit juice	£ 0.30
soup	£ 0.50
cold meat salad	£ 2.50
sausages (2)	£ 1.00
bacon & egg	£ 1.00
cod	£ 1.50
plaice	£ 2.00
portion of chips	£ 0.75
tea	£ 0.25
coffee	£ 0.35

all prices exclude VAT

figure 1.2

Figure 1.3 illustrates part of a railway timetable. The names of the stations are represented by groups of characters, the departure or arrival of a train by a single character **d** or **a**, and the times of departure or arrival of a train by numbers that represent the time of day.

Don't get the idea that data is always a group of characters followed by numbers. Figure 1.4 illustrates a bank cheque. The cheque number, bank clearing code and bank account number, written in magnetic characters at the bottom of the cheque, are all numbers. The payee name and the name of the account are represented by groups of characters. The amount in the box is represented as a number. The date can either be represented as a group of characters, or the values for day, month and year as numbers.

From these few examples it should be evident that data can take the form of whole numbers, such

Railway Timetable

Crewe	d				0639	0724	
Macclesfield	d				0641		0741
Stoke-on-Trent	d				0701	0710	0801
Stafford	d				0721	0747	0822
Wolverhampton	d			0643	0740	0807	0840
Birmingham New Street	a		0323	0702	0803	0830	0903
Birmingham New Street	d		0427	0706	0806		0906
Birmingham International	d			0716	0816	0858	0916
Coventry	d			0729	0829	0909	0929
Leamington Spa	a			0743	0843		0943
Banbury	a			0803	0903		1003
Oxford	a		0540	0826	0924		1024

figure 1.3

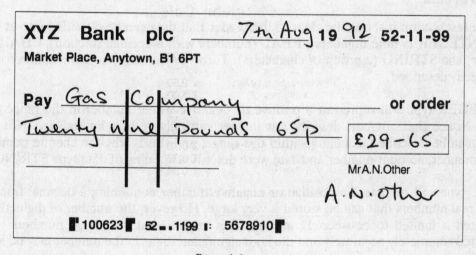

figure 1.4

as road distances and times of arrival or departure; numbers with a decimal fraction, such as amounts of money; single characters such as departure **d** or arrival **a** codes; and finally groups of characters such as place names, items of food and bank account names.

1.2 Types of data

Examine the data that has been presented in the previous four examples. In figure 1.1 the name of the town Keswick is composed from a group of characters and is known as a STRING data type. The number of miles, 15, on the road sign is a whole number and is known as an INTEGER data type.

The menu shown in figure 1.2 contains a mixture of data, the names of items of food and drink are of the data type STRING; the prices contain a decimal fraction and are numbers of data type REAL.

The railway timetable shown in figure 1.3 contains the names of the towns and cities of data type STRING, a single character to denote departure or arrival of data type CHAR and whole numbers that represent times, in a 24-hour clock format, of data type INTEGER.

The bank cheque shown in figure 1.4 contains the payee name and the name of the account of data type STRING. The amount shown in the box is REAL. However, despite the cheque number, bank clearing number and account number containing digits, they could each be represented as type STRING. This fact will become clearer after the next section on sizes of data. The date can either be three numbers representing day, month and year, each of data type INTEGER, or the complete date of type STRING. Note - a string can contain digits as well as letters and other characters.

1.3 Sizes of data

From the last section it should be clear to the reader that data can be classified into at least four types - INTEGER (whole numbers), REAL (numbers with a decimal fraction), CHAR (a single character) and STRING (a group of characters). Turbo Pascal uses the same names for the data types already described.

An INTEGER type will represent a positive or negative whole number in the range -32768 to +32767. Notice that numbers described as integer can only be of a limited size. Not all whole numbers can be described as falling within this range, and this is why the cheque number, bank clearing number, account number and date were described as being of data type STRING.

A REAL type will represent a positive or negative number containing a decimal fraction. The range of real numbers that can be stored is very large. However, the number of digits that can be represented is limited to between 11 and 12. This implies that very large numbers cannot be represented completely accurately and the least significant digits in the number may be lost!

The type declaration CHAR is used to denote a single character taken from the ASCII character set. This set is given in table 1.1 Notice that characters are not confined to letters of the alphabet, but can be digits and other symbols. Notice also that a numerical code, known as the ASCII code, is associated with each character, for example 'A' is coded 65, 'B' is coded 66, etc.

The type declaration STRING is used to represent a group of up to 255 characters.

1.4 Format of data

A syntax diagram, see figure 1.5, is a pictorial method of representing the format of components in a programming language. The direction of the arrowed lines indicates the order in which the diagram is to be read. In tracing through a diagram it is possible for the lines to branch into

Code	Character	Code	Character	Code	Character
000	NUL	043	+	086	V
001	SOH	044	,	087	W
002	STX	045	-	088	X
003	ETX	046	.	089	Y
004	EOT	047	/	090	Z
005	ENQ	048	0	091	[
006	ACK	049	1	092	\
007	BEL	050	2	093	]
008	BS	051	3	094	^
009	HT	052	4	095	_
010	LF	053	5	096	`
011	VT	054	6	097	a
012	FF	055	7	098	b
013	CR	056	8	099	c
014	SO	057	9	100	d
015	SI	058	:	101	e
016	DLE	059	;	102	f
017	DC1	060	<	103	g
018	DC2	061	=	104	h
019	DC3	062	>	105	i
020	DC4	063	?	106	j
021	NAK	064	@	107	k
022	STN	065	A	108	l
023	ETB	066	B	109	m
024	AN	067	C	110	n
025	EM	068	D	111	o
026	SUB	069	E	112	p
027	ESC	070	F	113	q
028	FS	071	G	114	r
029	GS	072	H	115	s
030	RS	073	I	116	t
031	US	074	J	117	u
032	space	075	K	118	v
033	!	076	L	119	w
034	"	077	M	120	x
035	#	078	N	121	y
036	$	079	O	122	z
037	%	080	P	123	{
038	&	081	Q	124		
039	'	082	R	125	}
040	(	083	S	126	~
041	)	084	T	127	del
042	*	085	U		

table 1.1 ASCII codes and characters

several directions. Such a branch shows there is a choice of components at that particular point in the diagram. Components on the diagram that are represented in circular or oval symbols are terminal components. These components, unlike components represented in square or rectangular symbols, cannot be represented by further syntax diagrams.

The formats of integer and real number are depicted by the syntax diagrams given in figure 1.5.

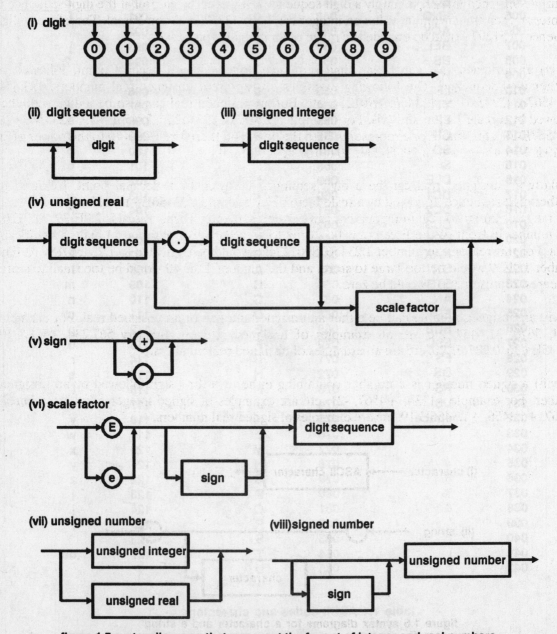

figure 1.5 syntax diagrams that represent the format of integer and real numbers

6

In (i) a digit is read to be any single decimal digit in the range 0 .. 9.

In (ii) a digit sequence is read to be a digit, possibly followed by another digit, possibly followed by another digit, etc, until the required sequence of digits is obtained. Therefore by definition the following examples all represent digit sequences: 5, 51, 513, 5139, 51297, etc.

In (iii) an unsigned integer is simply a digit sequence. However, be careful, if the digit sequence is an integer, then the maximum value an integer can be is 32767 in Turbo Pascal. Therefore, a digit sequence of 51297 would be outside the range of an integer type.

In (iv) an unsigned real can be an digit sequence, followed by a decimal point, followed by another digit sequence. The following examples all represent unsigned real numbers: 123.456, 12.345678, 12345.6789, 123456.78901234, etc. But an unsigned real can also be a digit sequence followed by a scale factor, see (vi). For example, 1234E26, 1234e26, 123456E+19, 123456e+19, 1234567E-20, etc. Note E or e represents 10 to the power of, therefore E26 is 10 to the power of 26, E+19 is 10 to the power of 19, E-20 is 10 to the power of -20.

Similarly an unsigned real can be a digit sequence followed by a decimal point, followed by another digit sequence, followed by a scale factor. For example 1.23456E+15, 1234.5678e-10, etc. The range of unsigned real numbers that can be represented in Turbo Pascal is 2.9E-39 .. 1.7E38. The number in front of the E can only be stored to an accuracy of between 11 and 12 significant digits. For this reason the number 1.234567890123456 would be truncated to 1.23456789010. The number 1.0E39 would be too large to store, and the number 1.0E-40 would be too small to store, its nearest representation would be zero.

In (vii) an unsigned number can be either an unsigned integer, or an unsigned real. For example, 1234, 5678, 31, 467, etc are all examples of unsigned integers. Similary 567.234, 456E+10, 1.2345E+36, 0.9876E-20, etc are all examples of unsigned real numbers.

In (viii) a signed number is a number containing either a + or - sign followed by an unsigned number. For example, -1234, +4567, -21, etc are examples of signed integer numbers, whereas -4.567, +1.3456, +1.3456E-19, etc are examples of signed real numbers.

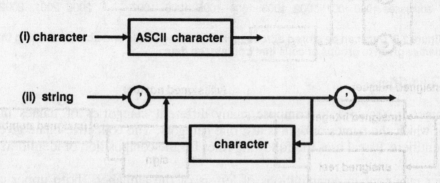

figure 1.6 syntax diagrams for a character and a string

From the syntax diagrams given in figure 1.6, a character is any character taken from the ASCII character set shown in table 1.1.

A string is delimited by single apostrophe characters. From the syntax diagram examples of strings could be '' (the null or empty string), 'a' (a string of length 1 is also compatible with a CHAR data type), 'abcdefg', etc.

1.5 Computer memory

The memory of a computer is made up from many millions of storage cells, and each cell has a unique numeric address. See figure 1.7.

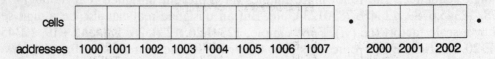

figure 1.7 A computer memory is made up from many storage cells, with each cell having a unique numeric address

Data may be thought of as occupying areas of the computer's memory in the same way as people occupy houses in a street. To distinguish different families in different houses we could use either the surname of the family or the number of the house. To distinguish data in different areas of memory we could give the data a name or use the numeric memory address where the data is stored. In the Pascal language it is much easier to refer to data by name and let the computer do the work of finding out where in memory the data is stored.

Figure 1.8 illustrates how data can be stored across the storage cells and accessed via the names given to the cells and not the address of the cells.

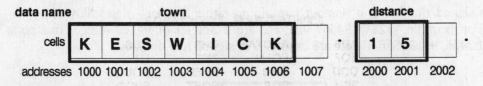

figure 1.8 Data can be stored across memory storage cells and accessed using the names given to groups of cells that contain the data.

1.6 Pascal identifiers

A programmer is required to compose many different categories of names in a computer program, of which the names of data is just one category. The collective name given to all these names is identifiers. Pascal uses the following rules for the composition of identifiers.

An identifier may contain combinations of letters of the alphabet, (both upper case A..Z and lower case a..z) and digits (0..9), provided the identifier begins with a letter. An identifier must not be the same as those Pascal words found in table 1.2. Identifiers can normally be of any length, however, Turbo Pascal only recognises up to 63 characters. Although upper and lower case letters can be used, Pascal does not distinguish between the two cases. Turbo Pascal allows embedded underscores _ as part of the identifier. A programmer should always compose the names of data so the names convey the meaning of the data. The identifiers *name*, *street*, *town*, *postcode* imply the meaning of the data that they represent, rather than identifiers N, S, T or P. When an identifier is constructed from more than one word, each word should either begin with an upper case letter, or be separated by an underscore, so that the identifier can be clearly read and its meaning understood. Examples of legal identifiers are SubTotal, VAT, total, rate_of_pay.

Reserved Words

AND	END	MAXINT	REPEAT
ARRAY	FILE	MOD	SET
BEGIN	FOR	NOT	THEN
CASE	FORWARD	OF	TO
CONST	FUNCTION	OR	TYPE
DIV	GOTO	PACKED	UNTIL
DO	IF	PROCEDURE	VAR
DOWNTO	IN	PROGRAM	WHILE
ELSE	LABEL	RECORD	WITH

Special Identifiers

BOOLEAN	NIL
CHAR	OUTPUT
FALSE	REAL
INPUT	TEXT
INTEGER	TRUE

Predefined Functions

ABS	ARCTAN	CHR	COS
EOF	EOLN	EXP	LN
ODD	ORD	PRED	ROUND
SIN	SQR	SQRT	SUCC
TRUNC			

Predefined Procedures

DISPOSE	GET	NEW	PUT
READ	READLN	RESET	REWRITE
WRITE	WRITELN		

table 1.2 words that must NOT be used as programmer defined identifiers

1.7 Data declaration

When investigating the data that is to be used in a computer program it can be helpful to document this information on a data analysis form as shown in figure 1.9. The form has been completed from the study of the four everyday situations presented earlier in the chapter. A description of the data helps to provide a clearer meaning of the identifiers being used. The data type is established and approximate sizes of data recorded. Where sizes of data cannot be predicted the maximum size for the data type has been recorded.

DATA ANALYSIS FORM			
description	identifier	data type	size
name of town	town	STRING	<=255 chars
distance to town in miles	distance	INTEGER	<=32767
item of food or drink	item	STRING	<=255 chars
price of item	price	REAL	<=2.50
name of town	town	STRING	<=255 chars
arrival or departure code	a_d_code	CHAR	1 char
time of day - 24 hour format	time	INTEGER	<=2359
cheque number	ChequeNumber	STRING	6 chars
clearing code number	ClearingCode	STRING	6 chars
account number	AccountNumber	STRING	7 chars
name of acount	name	STRING	<=255 chars
name cheque made out to	payee	STRING	<=255 chars
amount cheque made out for	amount	REAL	<=1,000,000.00
date cheque written	date	STRING	<=19 chars

figure 1.9 an example of the use of a data analysis form

A Pascal program can be divided into two areas, data declarations and instructions. The data declarations must appear before the instructions since they describe the type of data used by the instructions.

If the values of the data in the storage cells can be changed by the instructions in a computer program, then the values of the data vary, and the data identifiers are known as variable names. Figure 1.10 illustrates the syntax of a variable declaration in a Pascal program. The data declaration for such items must be headed by the word VAR. A data declaration contains the variable name followed by the data type.

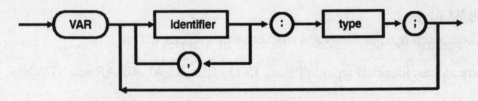

figure 1.10 syntax diagram to represent variable declarations

For example the data declaration for the road sign shown in figure 1.1 might be:

```
VAR
  NameOfTown   : STRING;
  distance     : INTEGER;
```

Similarly the data declarations for the menu shown in figure 1.2 might be:

```
VAR
  Item    : STRING;
  price   : REAL;
```

Notice that the declaration of the name of the cafe, the title and the last line of the menu and the currency sign have not been included since these are not variable quantities. Only the item of food and the price will vary according to the data being used.

The data declarations for the railway timetable shown in figure 1.3 might be:

```
VAR
  NameOfTown   : STRING;
  a_d_code     : CHAR;
  time         : INTEGER;
```

The heading has been ignored since this is not a variable quantity. Clearly the name of the town, arrival/ departure code and time do vary according to the data being used.

Finally, the data declarations for the bank cheque shown in figure 1.4, ignoring the name and address of the bank, and the amount in words, might be:

```
VAR
  ChequeNumber    : STRING;
  ClearingCode    : STRING;
  AccountNumber   : STRING;
  name            : STRING;
  payee           : STRING;
  amount          : REAL;
  date            : STRING;
```

1.8 Summary

● Data is composed from numbers and characters that represent facts.

● There are at least four data types in Pascal, INTEGER, REAL, CHAR and STRING.

● The size of data is limited by its type, and must fit between pre- defined ranges.

● Data must conform to set formats.

● A syntax diagram is used to denote the format of an item in a computer language.

● Data stored in the memory of a computer can be referenced through a data name invented by the programmer.

● Data names must conform to the rules for identifiers.

● A data analysis form should be used for documenting the description, name, type and size of all variables.

● All the variables used in a Pascal program must be declared, before they can be used by instructions contained in the program.

● Variable data declaration specifies the name of the data, followed by the type of the data.

1.9 Questions

1. From the illustrations in figures 1.11, 1.12 and 1.13 of items found in everyday life, discuss what you consider to be data, and show how the data is classified by type as variables declared in a Pascal program.

used cars for sale

Astra 1.4 L, 5 door, 91 (H), blue	£6750
BMW 316, 2 door, 87 (E), black	£6590
BMW 320i SE, 4 door, 88 (E), blue	£7990
Escort 1.6 Ghia Estate, 91 (J), silver	£9750
Fiesta 1.1 LX, 5 door, 91 (H), white	£6490
Granada 2.0 LXI, 90 (H), white	£6390
Jaguar 2.9 Auto, ABS, air con, 90 (G), grey	£12990
Nissan Sunny 1.6 GSX, 4 door, 89 (F), white	£5690
Sierra Sapphire 1.8 LX, 89 (F), white	£4990
Toyota Corolla, 89 (G), silver	£3990
VW Golf 1.6, 5 door, 87 (E), blue	£4790

figure 1.11

```
                                        XYZ  Bank  plc
Mr A.N.Other                            Market Place, Anytown, B1 6PT

                                        Statement  of  Account
```

1993 sheet 90 Account No. 5678910	DEBIT	CREDIT	BALANCE Credit C Debit D
JAN18 BALANCE BROUGHT FORWARD			550.50 C
JAN21 cheque 100642	55.86		494.64 C
JAN26 cheque 100644	10.08		484.56 C
JAN27 SWEET HOME BUILDING SOCIETY	280.14		204.42 C
JAN28 cheque 100643	51.69		152.73 C
FEB 1 SALARY		650.00	802.73 C
FEB 4 cheque 100645	38.11		764.62 C
FEB 8 GAS COMPANY	32.00		732.62 C
FEB 9 ELECTRICITY COMPANY	22.00		710.62 C
FEB10 cheque 100647	10.08		700.54 C
FEB11 cheque 100648	41.96		658.58 C
FEB15 SUNDRIES		15.00	673.58 C
FEB18 BALANCE CARRIED FORWARD			673.58 C

figure 1.12

Gas Bill

```
Mr   A.N.Other                          Date of bill
23  Beauchamp  Ave
Anytown                                 7  AUG  92
B1  6QT
```

Date of meter reading	Meter reading Present	Previous	Gas supplied cubic metres	KWh	Charges
7 AUG	7329E	7284	127.3	1361	21.31

BILLING PERIOD FROM 18.5.92 TO 7.8.92

81 DAYS STANDING CHARGE AT 10.3p PER DAY — 8.34

Amount Due £ 29. 65

figure 1.13

2. Identify the illegal variable names in the following list of identifiers. State why you think the names are illegal.

a. PriceOfBricks   b. net-pay   c. X1 d. cost of paper

e. ReadLn   f. ?X?Y   g. 1856AD

3. Describe the types of the following items of data.

a. 'OXFORD'	**b. -0.789**	**c. +156**	**d. 'X'**
e. 65456	**f. 65456.0**	**g. -329**	**h. -32768**
i. +32767	**j. +32768**	**k. 31851976.28**	

4. Using table 1.1 what are the ASCII codes of the following characters?

A M * a m / ? BEL NUL 9

5. Write the following numbers using the E notation for real numbers, such that there is only one non-zero digit to the left of the decimal point.

a. -874.458   b. +0.00123456   c. 123456789.0

6. State, giving reasons, why the following numbers cannot be stored as **REAL** numbers in Turbo Pascal.

a. 30.16E+38   b. 1234567890.1234567 c. -0.000456E-39

7. From the syntax diagram shown below, that represents a constant (a quantity that does not vary), list with examples all the posible formats of a constant.

constant

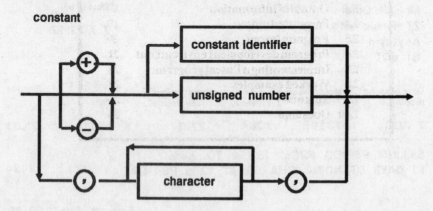

2.
Processing data

This chapter explains how to write instructions to input data into a computer, calculate and output results. This is the reader's introduction to writing simple computer programs. The necessary stages in transferring the program from the written word to a form the computer can recognise and understand is also examined.

2.1 Arithmetic

In section 1.5 of the previous chapter it was shown that data can be stored by name in the memory of a computer. Figure 2.1 illustrates numbers being stored by names A, B and C in three separate locations in memory.

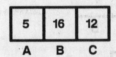

figure 2.1 numbers stored by name

The arithmetic operators + (addition) - (subtraction) * (multiplication) and / (division) can be used to make calculations on the stored numeric data. For example A := B + C would add the contents of B to the contents of C and store the result in A, destroying or overwriting the previous contents of A. Therefore, after the statement A := B + C had been executed by the computer the contents of A changed, and the result of the computation is shown in figure 2.2.

The symbol := is known as an assignment operator and must not be confused with the symbol = which has a different meaning in the Pascal language.

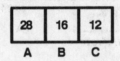

figure 2.2 result of the computation A:=B+C

Similar before and after situations can be applied to other computations as illustrated in figure 2.3.

The destination of a result will always be on the left-hand side of an assignment. Therefore, A:=9 implies that A is assigned the value 9. The statement 9:=A has no meaning since 9 is an illegal variable name. However, A:=B would imply that A is assigned the value of B, whereas, B:=A would imply that B is assigned the value of A.

Warning! Be careful about the declarations of data types in assignment statements.

Because integer numbers and real numbers are stored differently in the memory of a computer it is necessary to consider the data type of the left-hand variable in an assignment expression containing both integer and real numbers. A summary of the resultant types is given in figure 2.4.

However, there are exceptions to the summary given in figure 2.4. If an expression contains integers only, that are divided, for example 14/4, the result 3.5 is real, since this value cannot be stored as an integer.

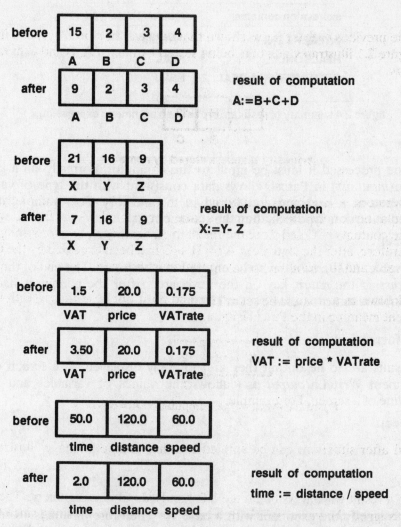

before

15	2	3	4
A	B	C	D

after

9	2	3	4
A	B	C	D

result of computation

A:=B+C+D

before

21	16	9
X	Y	Z

after

7	16	9
X	Y	Z

result of computation

X:=Y- Z

before

1.5	20.0	0.175
VAT	price	VATrate

after

3.50	20.0	0.175
VAT	price	VATrate

result of computation

VAT := price * VATrate

before

50.0	120.0	60.0
time	distance	speed

after

2.0	120.0	60.0
time	distance	speed

result of computation

time := distance / speed

figure 2.3 results of various computations on the contents of memory

If an integer result is required from the division of two integer values then use the Pascal function DIV. For example, 14 DIV 4 would give a result of 3 and not 3.5. However, if the remainder of an integer division is required then use the Pascal function MOD. For example, 14 MOD 4 gives the result remainder 2, after the integer division 14 divided by 4.

Furthermore, if the variables I and R are of type integer and real respectively, the assignment R:=I is valid, since a whole number can be stored in the format for a real number. However, the assignment I:=R is invalid since a real number containing a decimal fraction cannot be represented as an integer.

expression contains	resultant data type
INTEGERS ONLY	INTEGER
REALS ONLY	REAL
BOTH INTEGER & REAL	REAL

figure 2.4 summary of resultant types in an arithmetic expression

2.2 Input of data

Before data can be processed it must be input to the computer, normally via a keyboard. The statement **ReadLn**(*input list*) in Pascal, allows data consistent with the type of variables in the *input list*, to be typed at a keyboard and stored in the memory. For example, if the variable distance is declared to be data type real, then the statement

    ReadLn(distance)

would enable the value, *120.0 return*, say, to be entered at a keyboard. The end of the line of data is indicated by depressing the *return* key on the keyboard. After the computer had obeyed this statement the variable **distance** would be set at **120.0.**

2.3 Output of information

When data or results are to be output they are normally displayed on a screen or printed on paper. The statement **WriteLn**(*output list*) allows the values of variables and literals to be displayed on one line of a screen. For example,

    WriteLn(distance)

would display

1.2000000000E+02

where E is used to signify the exponent with a base 10. Therefore, E+02 is 10 squared, so the number is 1.2 x 100 = 120.

It is possible to output messages to a screen by replacing the output list by a string of characters (also known as a string literal). For example,

    WriteLn('Input distance to town ')

would display the prompt

input distance to town

on one line of the screen. After the execution of a WriteLn statement a new line is automatically generated.

A **WriteLn** statement without an output list will generate a blank line.

If it is necessary to suppress the generation of a new line then a **Write** statement can be used. For example the following statements:

```
Write('input distance to town ');
ReadLn(distance);
Write('input speed of travel ');
ReadLn(speed);
```

would result in the following display on the screen.

input distance to town 120.0
input speed of travel 60.0

where *120.0 return* and *60.0 return* have been typed in response to the prompts.

A list of variables and string literals, separated by commas, can be combined in the same output list of a WriteLn statement. For example,

```
WriteLn('distance travelled ', distance, 'average speed ', speed)
```

would display

distance travelled 1.2000000000E+02 average speed 6.0000000000E+01

on the screen.

2.4 Formatted output

The format of numeric data on a screen corresponds to the manner in which it is stored. In the example given in the previous section real numbers were displayed in two parts a decimal fraction known as a mantissa, and a scaling factor known as an exponent. This form of notation is not as common as that used to input the two real numbers 120.0 and 60.0. A further change can be made to the output list by specifying the field width (maximum number of characters including digits, decimal point and operational sign, that are to be displayed) and the number of decimal places to output. Thus **distance:8:2** would display a number with a field width of 8 characters and 2 decimal places. Similarly, **speed:4:1** would display a number with a field width of 4 characters with 1 decimal place.

```
WriteLn('distance travelled ', distance:8:2, 'average speed ', speed:4:1)
```

would display

distance travelled ss120.00 average speed 60.0

where **ss** represents two spaces displayed before the number to make up the field width to 8 characters. If the number to be output is of type integer, then only the field width need be declared. For example, if distance and speed had been declared as being integers, then the statement

```
WriteLn('distance travelled ', distance:6, 'average speed ', speed:4)
```

19

would display

distance travelled sss120 average speed ss60

2.5 Program layout

Figure 2.5 illustrates the syntax diagram for a Pascal program.

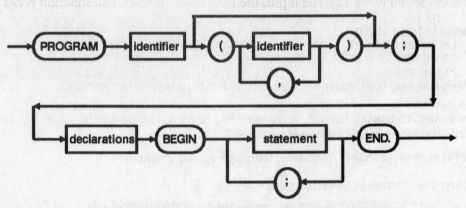

figure 2.5 syntax diagram for the layout of a Pascal program

Notice that a program begins with the reserved word PROGRAM followed by an identifier which represents the name of the program, followed by further identifiers enclosed between parenthesis (). The identifiers within parenthesis are the names of the standard text-file variables known as INPUT and OUTPUT which respectively represent a read-only file associated with the keyboard and a write-only file associated with the display. The reader needs only to remember that INPUT should be included if keyboard input is used; OUTPUT should be included if screen/ printer output is used; and both INPUT, OUTPUT should be included if keyboard input and screen/ printer output is required in the same program. For example a typical first line to a Pascal program might look like this.

PROGRAM TravelTime(INPUT, OUTPUT);

Notice the ; (semi-colon) at the end of the line to separate the opening line from the declarations. Variable declarations were covered in the previous chapter, and it is necessary to stress that all variables that are to be used in a program should normally be declared after the program heading and before the executable statements that the computer obeys. However, there are exceptions to this rule that will be explained later in the book. In a program to calculate the time it takes to travel a set distance at a known average speed the variable declarations might appear as follows.

VAR
  distance : INTEGER;
  speed   : INTEGER;
  time   : REAL;

Notice that VAR only appears once, and the declaration of each variable and its type is separated from the next by a ; (semi-colon).

The Pascal language allows program statements to be bracketed by the words BEGIN and END and all the statements between these reserved words will be executed in sequence by a computer. Notice that the statements are separated from each other by semi-colons, and the word END is terminated by a full stop. The following sequence of instructions will prompt for a distance from a destination and speed of travel to be input, the time taken to reach a destination is calculated, and the time is output.

```
BEGIN
    Write('Input distance to town ');
    ReadLn(distance);
    Write('input speed of travel ');
    ReadLn(speed);
    time := distance / speed;
    WriteLn('time taken to reach town is ', time:4:1, ' hours');
END.
```

2.6 Program development environment

After a computer program has been written it is transferred to a computer. This section briefly departs from the Pascal language, and investigates a typical computer environment for the development of Pascal programs.

Figure 2.6 illustrates a computer model containing the main memory, central processing unit (CPU), input, output and secondary storage units.

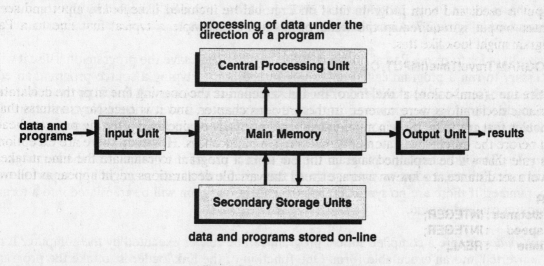

figure 2.6 a computer model

The main memory is used to temporarily store program instructions and data. A computer can only obey program instructions that are stored in the main memory.

The CPU consists of two sub-units, the arithmetic and logic unit (ALU) and the control unit. The ALU performs the processes of arithmetic, logical operations and comparisons on data. Whereas the control unit fetches the instructions from main memory, interprets and obeys them, and coordinates the flow of information about the system.

An input unit allows data and computer programs to be input into the computer model.

Since the main memory is only used to temporarily store programs and data, it is necessary to have secondary storage units to provide a permanent storage facility. Programs and data are transferred to and from the secondary storage units to the main memory only when they are required.

In order to transfer results from the main memory and secondary storage units to the outside world it is necessary to provide an output unit.

A typical hardware configuration to be found in a program development environment might be as follows.

Input Unit: keyboard.

Output Units: screen and printer.

Computer - includes CPU and main memory: A microcomputer such as an IBM PC or compatible.

Secondary Storage Units: 3.5" removable discs and fixed hard disc.

The phases that a Pascal program must undergo before it can be executed by the computer are summarised in figure 2.7. An explanation of this figure follows.

Editor: In order to type a Pascal program at the keyboard and save the program on a disc it will be necessary to run a program called an editor. In addition to typing a source program, an editor allows a program to be retrieved from disc and amended as necessary. A Pascal program is stored in text mode so that the programmer can read the program as it was written. No translation of the Pascal program to a form the computer can recognise has been necessary at this stage.

Compiler: This will check the program for the correct use of the grammar of the language. Any grammatical errors, known as syntax errors, that are found at this stage will be reported to the programmer. If there are no syntax errors present the program will be translated into a form the computer can understand.

Link/Loader: Before a compiled Pascal program can be run or executed by the computer it must be converted into an executable form. One function of the link/loader is to take the program as

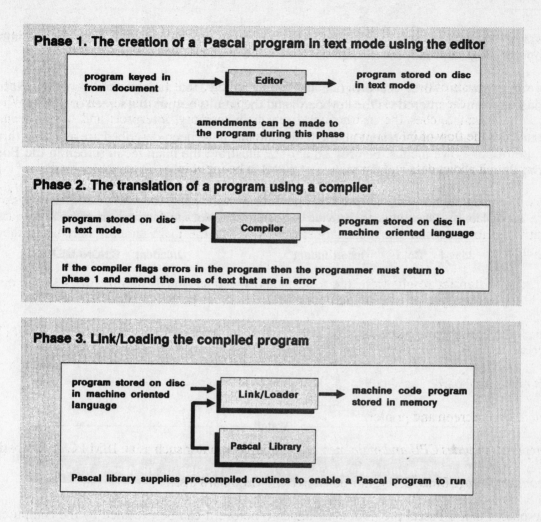

Phase 1. The creation of a Pascal program in text mode using the editor

program keyed in from document → Editor → program stored on disc in text mode

amendments can be made to the program during this phase

Phase 2. The translation of a program using a compiler

program stored on disc in text mode → Compiler → program stored on disc in machine oriented language

If the compiler flags errors in the program then the programmer must return to phase 1 and amend the lines of text that are in error

Phase 3. Link/Loading the compiled program

program stored on disc in machine oriented language → Link/Loader → machine code program stored in memory

Pascal Library

Pascal library supplies pre-compiled routines to enable a Pascal program to run

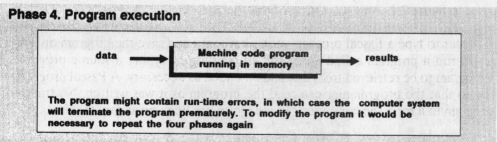

Phase 4. Program execution

data → Machine code program running in memory → results

The program might contain run-time errors, in which case the computer system will terminate the program prematurely. To modify the program it would be necessary to repeat the four phases again

figure 2.7 the four phases of program development

translated by the compiler and combine it with any necessary software to enable the program to run. For example, input and output routines that are supplied by the system will need linking into the program to allow data to be input at a keyboard and results displayed on a screen. The complete program, now in a form that the computer can recognise, is then loaded into the computer's memory ready for execution.

Program execution: After the program has been loaded into memory and program execution begins, data can be entered via the keyboard, and the results output to a screen or printer.

In the Turbo Pascal environment all the functions that have been described are available through the use of pull-down menus. Figures 2.8 and 2.9 illustrate the main menu screen in the Borland Turbo Pascal environment, and a sample of pull-down menus.

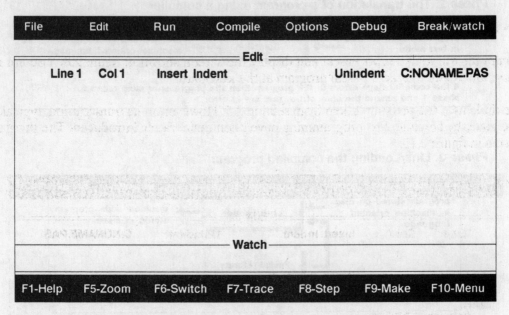

figure 2.8 the Borland Turbo Pascal main menu screen

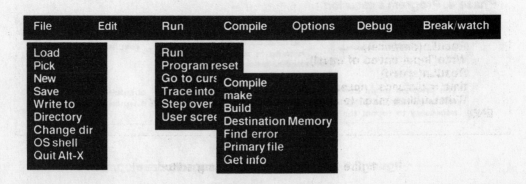

figure 2.9 a sample of pull-down menus in the Borland Turbo Pascal environment

The program can be operated by pressing the function key 'F10' and invoking pull-down menu for the select the 'file' and option, and type in the full name, i.e. on the start the program. This

2.7 Implementing a Pascal program

Assuming that the reader is using a Turbo Pascal environment, the following stages are necessary to implement a Pascal program.

Enter the Turbo Pascal environment by changing to the directory containing this environment.

C:\>cd TP

Type the word TURBO at the prompt.

C:\TP>TURBO

The computer will load Turbo Pascal and display the screen shown in figure 2.8. You are now in the *editor*, and ready to type a Pascal program at the keyboard.

This example uses the program taken from section 2.5. However, in its transcription, typical errors that are made by beginners to programming have been deliberately introduced. The program has been listed in figure 2.10.

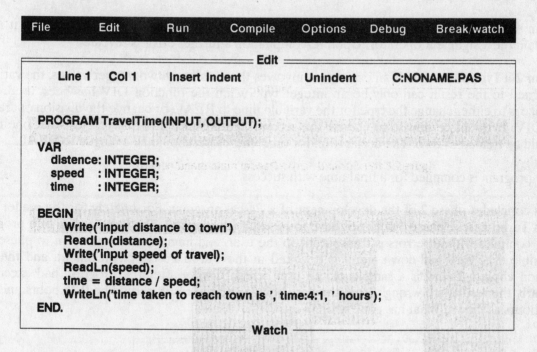

```
  File        Edit        Run      Compile     Options    Debug     Break/watch
───────────────────────────────────── Edit ─────────────────────────────────────
    Line 1   Col 1      Insert Indent              Unindent      C:NONAME.PAS

 PROGRAM TravelTime(INPUT, OUTPUT);

 VAR
    distence: INTEGER;
    speed   : INTEGER;
    time    : INTEGER;

 BEGIN
     Write('input distance to town')
     ReadLn(distance);
     Write('input speed of travel);
     ReadLn(speed);
     time = distance / speed;
     WriteLn('time taken to reach town is ', time:4:1, ' hours');
 END.
───────────────────────────────────── Watch ────────────────────────────────────
```

figure 2.10 program input using editor

The program can be saved on disc by pressing the function key F10, and invoking pull-down menu for File. Select the Write to option, and type a suitable name for the storing the program. This concludes phase 1 and the program is now ready for compilation.

The *Compile* pull-down menu is selected and the compile option is envoked.

The following error message will appear on the screen

Error 85: ";" expected, and the screen cursor will be pointing at the ReadLn(distance) statement. This can be very misleading since the error occurred on the previous line. You may notice that the Write statement has not been separated from the ReadLn statement by a semi-colon. Remember the semi-colon is a statement separator. Having corrected this error, you re- compile the program only to find another error.

Error 3: Unknown identifier, with the screen cursor pointing at the word distance. Remember ALL identifiers must be declared before they can be used in executable statements. By inspecting the declaration of distance you should notice that distance has been spelt incorrectly. Having edited the declaration for distance, the program can again be recompiled. This time the error message reads:

Error 8: String constant exceeds line, and the screen cursor is pointing at the end of the second prompt Write('input speed of travel); The closing ' string delimiter has been omitted. This line is corrected and the program is once again re-compiled. Yet another error message is listed as:

Error 91: ":=" expected. Clearly the equals sign in the assignment statement is wrong it must contain the assignment operator. Upon re-compilation a further error is revealed.

Error 26: Type mismatch. If an expression involves the division of two integer values, the variable assigned to the result can only be an integer type when the function DIV has been used. The choice is to either change the type for the variable time to REAL, or change the division operator / to DIV. If would be unwise to choose the second option, since any times of less that one hour would be treated as zero. The declaration for time, therefore, should be changed to REAL.

The program is compiled for a final time with success.

This concludes phase 2 of the development of a Pascal program. Fortunately for the reader who uses Turbo Pascal, phase 3 does not have to be explicitly invoked. The *link/ loading* of a program that compiles without errors is transparent to the user, and immediate progression to phase 4 is possible. The *Run* pull-down menu is envoked in the Turbo Pascal environment, and the run option chosen. Below is a sample of the user screen display after the program had executed. Clearly the results are wrong. From the data being used the result should be 0.25 hours and not 0.3 hours as shown. What has gone wrong?

```
input distance to town  15
input speed of travel  60
time taken to reach town is  0.3 hours
```

This is not so much an error, but a mistake in the use of the output format for the number of hours. The format used, only caters for 1 decimal place, yet to display the correct answer requires two decimal places. Since the correct answer is 0.25, the computer has rounded the answer to 0.3, before displaying the value with one decimal place.

The correct version of the program follows, together with specimen output. Notice that comments have been added to the program. Any text contained between braces { } is treated in Pascal as a comment. The compiler ignores all comment lines. In this example two types of comments have been given. The first appears after the program heading and describes the purpose of the program. The second appears at the end on the program as an indication that program TravelTime has ended. This second use of a comment might seem trivial, but is very useful when several program components have endings, as the reader will see later in the book.

```
PROGRAM TravelTime(INPUT, OUTPUT);
{
program to calculate and output the time in hours, to travel a distance input in miles,
at an average speed input in m.p.h.
}

VAR
    distance : INTEGER;
    speed    : INTEGER;
    time     : REAL;
BEGIN
    Write('input distance to town ');
    ReadLn(distance);
    Write('input speed of travel ');
    ReadLn(speed);
    time := distance / speed;
    WriteLn('time taken to reach town is ', time:4:2, ' hours');
END. {TravelTime}
```

```
input distance to town  15
input speed of travel  60
time taken to reach town is  0.25 hours
```

2.8 Worked examples

The following examples show how data can be input at a keyboard, under the direction of prompts on a screen; processed according to the nature of the problem and the results displayed on a screen. The examples illustrate a simple order involved in processing data:

input data
process data
output results

The reader is recommended to keep this order in mind when attempting to write programs.

Input is not confined to numbers. The previous program can be modified to include the name of the destination being input. This name can then be used in further prompts in the same program.

```
PROGRAM TravelTime(INPUT, OUTPUT);
{
program to calculate and output the time in hours, to travel a distance input in miles,
at an average speed input in m.p.h.
}
VAR
    town     : STRING;
    distance : INTEGER;
    speed    : INTEGER;
    time     : REAL;

BEGIN
    Write('input name of town ');
    ReadLn(town);
    Write('input distance to ', town, ' ');
    ReadLn(distance);
    Write('input speed of travel ');
    ReadLn(speed);
    time := distance / speed;
    WriteLn('time taken to reach ', town, ' is ', time:4:2, ' hours');
END. {TravelTime}
```

```
input name of town Keswick
input distance to Keswick 15
input speed of travel 60
time taken to reach Keswick is 0.25 hours
```

The following program demonstrates the input of the names and prices of three newspapers, and calculates and outputs the total cost and average price of the papers.

```
PROGRAM newspapers(INPUT, OUTPUT);
{
program to input the names and prices of three newspapers, calculate and output the total cost
and average price of the papers
}
VAR
    NamePaper1, NamePaper2, NamePaper3   : STRING;
    PricePaper1, PricePaper2, PricePaper3 : INTEGER;
    TotalCost                             : INTEGER;
    average                               : REAL;
```

```
BEGIN
    {Input name and price of three newspapers}
    Write('name of first newspaper ');        ReadLn(NamePaper1);
    Write('price of ', NamePaper1, ' ');       ReadLn(PricePaper1);
    Write('name of second newspaper ');        ReadLn(NamePaper2);
    Write('price of ', NamePaper2, ' ');       ReadLn(PricePaper2);
    Write('name of third newspaper ');         ReadLn(NamePaper3);
    Write('price of ', namepaper3, ' ');       ReadLn(PricePaper3);

    {calculate total cost and average price of newspapers}
    TotalCost := PricePaper1 + PricePaper2 + PricePaper3;
    average := TotalCost / 3;

    {output values for the total cost and average price of newspapers}
    WriteLn('total cost of three newspapers is ', TotalCost:4, 'p');
    WriteLn('average price of newspapers is ', average:6:0, 'p');
END. {newspapers}
```

```
name of first newspaper Globe
price of Globe 40
name of second newspaper Mercury
price of Mercury 50
name of third newspaper Courier
price of Courier 60
total cost of three newspapers is 150p
average cost of newspapers is      50p
```

The menu provided by the Greasy Spoon Cafe was illustrated in the previous chapter (figure 1.2). If meals are categorised into three courses as starter, main course and beverage, then the next program will allow the name and price of items for each course to be input and a final bill to be output that includes the sub-total, value added tax at 17.5% and total for the meal. The motto of the Greasy Spoon Cafe is "chips with everything", so you are also billed for a portion of chips whether you eat them or not!

```
PROGRAM meal(INPUT, OUTPUT);
{
program to input the name and cost of items of food in a cafe, and output the bill for the meal
}
VAR
    starter, MainCourse, beverage        : STRING;
    PriceStarter, PriceMain, PriceBeverage : REAL;
    PriceChips                           : REAL;
    SubTotal                             : REAL;
    total                                : REAL;
    VAT                                  : REAL;
```

```
BEGIN
    {input name and price of starter, main course and beverage}
    Write('starter? ');                  ReadLn(starter);
    Write('price of ', starter, ' ');    ReadLn(PriceStarter);
    Write('main course? ');              ReadLn(MainCourse);
    Write('price of ', MainCourse, ' '); ReadLn(PriceMain);
    Write('beverage? ');                 ReadLn(beverage);
    Write('price of ', beverage, ' ');   ReadLn(PriceBeverage);

    {process sub total, vat and total}
    PriceChips:=0.75;
    SubTotal:=PriceStarter+PriceMain+PriceChips+PriceBeverage;
    VAT:=0.175*SubTotal;
    total:=SubTotal+VAT;

    {output bill for meal}
    WriteLn; WriteLn; WriteLn('G r e a s y  S p o o n  C a f e'); WriteLn;
    WriteLn(starter);
    WriteLn(PriceStarter:30:2);
    WriteLn(MainCourse);
    WriteLn(PriceMain:30:2);
    WriteLn('portion of chips');
    WriteLn(PriceChips:30:2);
    WriteLn(beverage);
    WriteLn(PriceBeverage:30:2);  WriteLn;
    WriteLn('SUBTOTAL                ',SubTotal:20:2);
    WriteLn('VAT                     ',VAT:20:2);
    WriteLn('TOTAL                   ',total:20:2);
END. {meal}
```

```
starter? soup
price of soup 0.50
main course? cold meat salad
price of cold meat salad 2.50
beverage? coffee
price of coffee 0.35

Greasy  Spoon  Cafe

soup
                        0.50
cold meat salad
                        2.50
portion of chips
                        0.75
coffee
                        0.35

SUBTOTAL                4.10
VAT                     0.72
TOTAL                   4.82
```

In this program the rate of value added tax (VAT) is a constant figure of 0.175 or 17.5%. Similarly the price of chips is always £0.75 and is added to every bill. Pascal will allow all constants to be declared in a program before the variable declarations. The format for a constant declaration is given in figure 2.11.

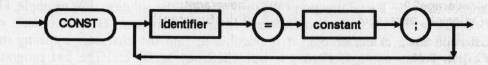

figure 2.11 syntax diagram for a constant declaration

The necessary amendments to the previous program to cater for the use of constants follows.

```
PROGRAM meal(INPUT, OUTPUT);
{
program to input the name and cost of items of food in a cafe, and output the bill for the meal
}
CONST
    VATrate = 0.175;
    PriceChips = 0.75;
```

In the program the line **PriceChips:=0.75;** is deleted, and the line **VAT:=0.175*SubTotal;** is replaced by **VAT:= VATrate*SubTotal;** Clearly if the rate of VAT or the price of chips changed, the only modifications required to the program are to the declarations of these constants. Any executable statements that use the constants will not need to be altered.

Continuing on the theme of introducing constant values into a program. The next program displays the Morse code for SOS. Since the Morse code is composed from dots and dashes it makes sense to include two constants dot and dash and a third constant space to delimit the codes. Notice in the program heading that only OUTPUT is defined since there is no keyboard input into the program.

```
PROGRAM morse(OUTPUT);
{
program to display the Morse code for SOS
}
CONST
    dot='.';
    dash='-';
    space='';
BEGIN
    Write('Morse code for SOS is ');
    WriteLn(dot, dot, dot, space, dash, dash, dash, space, dot, dot, dot);
END. {morse}
```

```
Morse code for SOS is . . . – – – . . .
```

Refer to chapter one, table 1.1 ASCII codes and characters. If you want to find the ASCII code for a character then the Pascal function ORD will provide the solution. For example, ORD('A') = 65, ORD('B') = 66, etc. Similarly there exists an inverse function CHR, such that if you know the ASCII code for a character then it is possible to find the character by using the Pascal function CHR. For example, CHR(65) = 'A', CHR(66) = 'B', etc. The last program of this section demonstrates the use of the functions ORD and CHR. A character is input at the keyboard and its ASCII code is displayed, followed by an ASCII code being input at the keyboard and the corresponding character is displayed. Notice from the table 1.1 that all the characters from code 0 to code 32 are not easily recognisable as characters that can be displayed on a screen. For this reason the user of the program is advised to input an ASCII code in the range 33 to 126 only.

```pascal
PROGRAM ascii(INPUT, OUTPUT);
{
program to input a single character and display its ASCII code, then input an ASCII
code and display the corresponding character
}
VAR
    character   : CHAR;
    code        : INTEGER;
BEGIN
    Write('input a single character ');  ReadLn(character);
    code := ORD(character);
    WriteLn('ASCII code for ', character, ' is ', code:3); WriteLn;

    Write('input an ASCII code in the range 33 to 126 '); ReadLn(code);
    character := CHR(code);
    WriteLn('character with ASCII code ', code:3, ' is ', character);
END. {ascii}
```

```
input a single character R
ASCII code for R is 82

input an ASCII code in range 33 to 126  64
character with ASCII code 64 is @
```

2.9 Summary

● Arithmetic can be used on the contents of the memory locations, allowing computations to be made on numeric data.

● Numbers can be added, subtracted, multiplied and divided by using the operators +, -, * and / respectively.

● When two integers are divided and an integer result is required, then use the function DIV, to calculate an integer quotient and the function MOD to calculate an integer remainder.

● The result of a computation is assigned to a variable using the := assignment operator.

● The resultant data type of a computation is dependent upon the data types being computed, however, there can be exceptions to the rules when integer division is used.

● Data is input at run-time, via a keyboard, in response to a ReadLn statement.

● Information or results are output from a program to a screen or printer using a WriteLn statement.

● Both strings and numbers can be output in the same WriteLn statement.

● The format of displaying both integers and real numbers can be controlled in a WriteLn statement.

● Quantities that do not vary during the running of a program can be declared as constants in a CONST statement, at the beginning of a program.

● The names of the constants should be used in the program and not their literal values.

● Constants must be declared before variables.

● All variables must be declared in a VAR statements before they can be used in the program.

● A semi-colon is used to **separate** statements in a Pascal program.

● The default files INPUT and OUTPUT should be declared in the heading of a program to allow for keyboard input and screen output respectively.

● A typical hardware configuration consists of keyboard (input device), screen and/ or printer (output devices), a floppy disc/ or hard disc unit (secondary storage devices), a main memory and a central processing unit.

● The software required in an environment for writing Pascal programs would typically contain an editor, compiler and link/ loader.

2.10 Questions

1. What are the values of the following variables after the execution of the respective assignments?

a. B := A;   A B C D
   C := A;   36 98 45 29
   D := A;

b. D := A + B + C + D;   A B C D
                          10 14 29 36

c. A := B - 2;   A B
              17 50

d. Y := X - Y;   X Y
              19 32

e. Z := X * Y;   X Y Z
              18 3 27

f. B := B / A;   A   B
              12.5 25.0

g. X := A DIV B;   A B X
                16 3 25

h. Y := C MOD D;   C D Y
                18 5 2

2. (a) Write a program to display the message 'Hello World' on the screen.

(b) Write a program to input a short message of your choice and display the message on the screen.

3. Write a program to store the numbers 5 and 9 as integer variables A and B respectively. Compute the sum, difference, product, integer quotient and remainder of these variables taken in the order A+B, A-B, A*B, A DIV B, A MOD B, and display the results on a screen.

4. Write a program to input your name, height in inches and weight in stones; convert the height to centimetres and weight to kilogrammes and display the following results. Note: 1 inch = 2.54 cm and 1 stone = 6.364 Kg.

> PERSONAL DETAILS
> NAME: Bert Smith
> HEIGHT (cm): 180
> WEIGHT (Kg): 75

5. Write a program to input a temperature in degrees Fahrenheit and display the equivalent

temperature in degrees Centigrade. The formula for conversion is: Centigrade = (Fahrenheit-32)*(5/9).

6. Write a program to input the length and width of a rectangular-shaped garden, calculate the area of the garden and the cost of turfing a lawn, if a 0.5m border is left around the perimeter of the garden. Assume the cost of turf is £0.75 per square metre. Display the result of these calculations.

7. Write a program to input an amount of money as a whole number, for example £157, and display an analysis of the minimum number of £20, £10, £5 notes and £1 coins that make up this amount. Hint: use the DIV and MOD functions.

8. Write a program to input the length, width and depths at the deepest and shallowest ends of a rectangular swimming pool. Calculate the volume of water required to fill the pool and display this volume.

9. Write a program to input a character in the range 0 to 9, convert the mode of storage to an integer, multiply the value by pi (3.14159) and output the result. Hint: use the ORD function to obtain the value of the ASCII code, for example ORD('0') = 48. Thus integer 0 = ORD('0')-48.

10. In each of the following questions you are expected to write program, constant and data declarations to fit the sequence of instructions given. When you have completed the declarations for each program, file, compile and run the programs on your computer.

a. The instruction sequence calculates the arithmetic mean of three integers and displays the result to an accuracy of two decimal places.

```
BEGIN
    Write('Input three integers separated by spaces e.g. 2 5 7');
    WriteLn('then press the RETURN key');
    ReadLn(x,y,z);
    mean:=(x+y+z)/numbers;
    WriteLn('arithmetic mean of integers = ', mean:10:2);
END. {C2Q10a}
```

b. The instruction sequence calculates the surface area and volume of a sphere.

```
BEGIN
    Write('Input integer value for the radius of the sphere =>');
    ReadLn(radius);
    SurfaceArea:=4*pi*radius*radius;
    volume:=SurfaceArea*radius/3;
    WriteLn('surface area of sphere =',SurfaceArea:10:2);
    WriteLn('volume of sphere =',volume:10:2);
END. {C2Q10b}
```

2. Processing data

c. The instruction sequence prepares a sales invoice.

```
BEGIN
    WriteLn('SALES INVOICE'); WriteLn; WriteLn;
    Write('Input cost of item 1');ReadLn(item1);
    Write('Input cost of item 2');ReadLn(item2);
    Write('Input cost of item 3');ReadLn(item3);
    SubTotal:=item1+item2+item3;
    Tax:=SubTotal*VAT;
    total:=SubTotal+Tax;
    WriteLn('Sub Total', SubTotal:10:2);
    WriteLn('VAT @ 17.5%', Tax:10:2);
    WriteLn('Total ', Total:10:2);
END. {C2Q10c}
```

3.
Making decisions

A computer program written as a sequence of instructions is fine for certain solutions to problems, but often there will be a need to make decisions in a program. This chapter looks at how to select different instructions depending upon the decisions being made.

Contents

3.1 If .. then

Consider the following simple program which informs the user of what garment to wear depending on whether it is raining or not.

```
PROGRAM weather(INPUT, OUTPUT);
{
program to demonstrate the IF .. THEN .. statement
}
VAR
    reply     : STRING;
    garment : STRING;
BEGIN
    garment := 'overcoat';
    Write('is it raining outside? answer yes or no ');
    ReadLn(reply);

    IF reply = 'yes' THEN
        garment := 'raincoat';
    {END IF}

    WriteLn('before you go out today take your ', garment);
END. {weather}
```

When the program is run twice the output appears as shown below.

```
is it raining outside? answer yes or no no
before you go out today take your overcoat

is it raining outside? answer yes or no yes
before you go out today take your raincoat
```

In tracing through the program the following operations take place.

The string variable **garment** is assigned the value **overcoat**. The user is then requested to input whether it is raining or not. If the answer to the question is **yes**, then the value of **garment** is changed to **raincoat**. However, if the answer to the question is **no**, then the value of **garment** remains unaltered. Finally the user is advised the type of garment to take before venturing outdoors.

When assigning a value to a string variable the string must be enclosed between apostrophes, for example **garment:='overcoat'**. However, when typing a string value at a keyboard the string is NOT enclosed between apostrophes, for example *is it raining outside? answer yes or no* **yes.**

In the program it has been possible to ask a question, and depending upon the answer, select an alternative statement for the computer to execute. This is possible by using the if..then statement

```
IF reply = 'yes' THEN
    garment := 'raincoat';
{END IF}
```

The expression **reply = 'yes'** is known as a Boolean expression, since it will either equate to TRUE (when the reply is equal to yes) or FALSE (when the reply is NOT equal to yes, therefore by implication may be equal to no). Only when the Boolean expression equates to TRUE will the statement immediately after the reserved word THEN be executed by the computer. If the Boolean expression equates to FALSE, the computer will ignore the statement after THEN and branch to the next executable statement after the comment {END IF}.

The end of the IF .. THEN statement, as far as the computer is concerned, follows the ; (semicolon) at the end of the statement **garment:='raincoat'**. The use of the comment {END IF} clearly indicates the end of the statement to the programmer, but like all comments is ignored by the computer. The reader should adopt the style of marking the endings of such statements, since it improves the readability of a program.

3.2 If .. then .. else

The syntax diagram in figure 3.1 illustrates that there is more to the if..then statement than was indicated in the previous section.

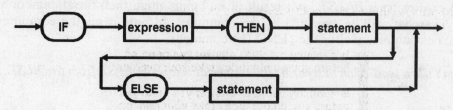

figure 3.1 syntax of an IF .. THEN .. ELSE statement

Consider the following modification to the previous program to include the statement if..then..else.

```
PROGRAM weather(INPUT, OUTPUT);
{
program to demonstrate the IF .. THEN .. ELSE statement
}
VAR
    reply    : STRING;
    garment  : STRING;
BEGIN
    Write('is it raining outside? answer yes or no ');
    ReadLn(reply);
```

```
    IF reply = 'yes' THEN
        garment := 'raincoat'
    ELSE
        garment := 'overcoat';
    {END IF}
    WriteLn('before you go out today take your ', garment);
END. {weather}
```

The function of the program is exactly the same as before. If it was executed using the same data as the first program then there would be no change in the output.

There are two differences in the construction of the program. Firstly there has been no initial assignment to the string variable **garment**, and secondly an if..then ..else statement of the form

```
IF reply = 'yes' THEN
    garment := 'raincoat'
ELSE
    garment := 'overcoat';
{END IF}
```

has replaced the if .. then statement in the previous program. The manner in which this statement functions is very straightforward. If the result of the Boolean expression **reply = 'yes'** is TRUE then the statement after THEN **garment := 'raincoat'** will be executed. However, if the result of the Boolean expression is FALSE, as a result of **no** being input, then the statement after ELSE **garment := 'overcoat'** will be executed by the computer. In both cases the computer will then branch to the next statement after the {END IF} comment.

Warning! Don't use a semi-colon to separate the statement before the ELSE from the ELSE.

3.3 Nested if 's

The statement that follows THEN and/or ELSE can also be an if statement. In the previous examples if the weather had been warm then wearing either a raincoat or an overcoat could prove to be very uncomfortable. If a second item of data is included about the temperature then it is possible to more accurately specify what to wear whether it is raining or not.

If it is raining and the temperature is less than 15 degrees Centigrade then wear a raincoat, otherwise if it is warmer then take an umbrella. However, if it is not raining and the temperature is less than 15 degrees Centigrade then wear an overcoat otherwise if it is warmer then wear a jacket. The program has been reconstructed to take these new facts into account. The outer if..then..else statement is used to determine which path to take depending upon whether it is raining. The inner if..then..else statements are used to determine which path to take depending upon the temperature.

Notice also the use of the relational operator in the expression **temperature < 15**. The relational operator **<** means *less than*. A list of relational operators that can be used in Boolean expressions is given in figure 3.2.

```
PROGRAM weather(INPUT, OUTPUT);
{
program to demonstrate nested IF .. THEN .. ELSE statements
}
VAR
    garment        : STRING;
    reply          : STRING;
    temperature    : INTEGER;
BEGIN
    Write('what is the temperature outside today? ');
    ReadLn(temperature);
    Write('is it raining outside? answer yes or no ');
    ReadLn(reply);

    IF reply = 'yes' THEN
        IF temperature < 15 THEN
            garment := 'raincoat'
        ELSE
            garment := 'umbrella'
        {END IF}
    ELSE
        IF temperature < 15 THEN
            garment := 'overcoat'
        ELSE
            garment := 'jacket';
        {END IF}
    {END IF}

    WriteLn('before you go out today take your ', garment);
END. {weather}
```

The results from executing this program four times follow.

```
what is the temperature outside today? 10
is it raining outside? answer yes or no yes
before you go out today take your  raincoat

what is the temperature outside today? 10
is it raining outside? answer yes or no no
before you go out today take your  overcoat

what is the temperature outside today? 15
is it raining outside? answer yes or no yes
before you go out today take your  umbrella

what is the temperature outside today? 15
is it raining outside? answer yes or no no
before you go out today take your  jacket
```

41

operator	meaning
>	greater than
<	less then
=	equal to
>=	greater than or equal to
<=	less than or equal to
<>	not equal to

figure 3.2 relational operators used in Boolean expressions

In the program, after both the temperature and reply have been input, if the Boolean expression **reply = 'yes'** is TRUE, then the statement after THEN will be obeyed. But this is another **if** statement! If the Boolean expression **temperature < 15** is TRUE then the statement after THEN **garment := 'raincoat'** will be executed, however, if the Boolean expression **temperature < 15** is FALSE then the statement after ELSE **garment := 'umbrella'** will be executed. In either case the computer will then branch to the next executable statement after the {END IF} comment of the outer if .. then .. else statement. If the Boolean expression **reply = 'yes'** is FALSE, then the statement after ELSE, in the outer if..then..else, will be obeyed, and if the Boolean expression **temperature < 15** is TRUE then the statement after THEN **garment := 'overcoat'** will be executed, however, if the Boolean expression **temperature < 15** is FALSE then the statement after ELSE **garment := 'jacket'** will be executed.

Look at the use of ; (semicolon) statement separators in these if..then..else statements, and try to understand when a semicolon is used, and when it is not. *Remember a semicolon is a statement separator*. However, if..then and if..then.. else are both statements. If a semicolon is used after a statement embedded within a selection statement, then the syntax of the selection statement is violated. For example,

```
IF temperature < 15 THEN
    garment := 'raincoat';
ELSE
    garment := 'umbrella';
{END IF}
```

would be wrong, and would cause the syntax error message **Error 113: Error in statement** to be flagged. The ; after the statement **garment:= 'raincoat'** has the effect of splitting the if .. then .. else statement into two separate statements which is syntactically wrong.

Consider the punctuation within the nested if .. then .. else statements.

```
IF reply = 'yes' THEN
    IF temperature < 15 THEN
        garment := 'raincoat'
    ELSE
        garment := 'umbrella'
    {END IF}
ELSE
```

```
    IF temperature < 15 THEN
        garment := 'overcoat'
    ELSE
        garment := 'jacket';
    {END IF}
  {END IF}
```

The only semicolon appears at the end of the last statement in the nested statements, **garment :=
'jacket'**. If a semicolon was to appear after any other statement it would have the effect of
dividing the appropriate if .. then .. else statement into two separate parts, and hence violate the
syntax of the if .. then .. else statement.

Warning! pay particular attention to the use of semi-colons in if .. then .. else statements.

3.4 Boolean data type

In the previous example how would the computer cater for data being input that did not match
either *yes* or *no* in response to a reply? If the reply was *don't know* then the Boolean expression
reply = 'yes' would be false and the computer would assign **overcoat** to the variable **garment** if the
temperature was less than fifteen degrees or would assign **jacket** to the variable **garment** if the
temperature was warmer. This is clearly an undesirable feature of the program, and it is the
responsibility of the programmer to trap any invalid data and report the exceptional
circumstances to the user of the program.

The next program traps and reports on data being input that does not conform to the reply *yes* or
no. The program introduces a new data type whose values are FALSE or TRUE only. This data
type is known as a BOOLEAN type. A variable **error**, has been declared as being BOOLEAN,
which means that the values FALSE or TRUE can be assigned to it. In the program the variable
error is initialised to FALSE on the assumption that no invalid data will be input. However, as
soon as invalid data is recognised, the value of **error** is changed to TRUE.

Since error is of type BOOLEAN and only has the values FALSE or TRUE assigned to it, the
variable may be used in place of a Boolean expression. Notice in the last segment of the program
code that if there has been an error, the message of what garment to take is suppressed and
replaced by a data error message.

```
PROGRAM weather(INPUT, OUTPUT);
{
program to demonstrate the use of a Boolean variable
}
VAR
    garment        : STRING;
    reply          : STRING;
    temperature    : INTEGER;
    error          : BOOLEAN;
BEGIN
    Write('what is the temperature outside today? ');
```

```
      ReadLn(temperature);
      Write('is it raining outside? answer yes or no ');
      ReadLn(reply);

      error := FALSE;

      IF reply = 'yes' THEN
          IF temperature < 15 THEN
              garment := 'raincoat'
          ELSE
              garment := 'umbrella'
          {END IF}
      ELSE
          IF reply = 'no' THEN
              IF temperature < 15 THEN
                  garment := 'overcoat'
              ELSE
                  garment := 'jacket'
              {END IF}
          ELSE                    {implies reply has not been input as either yes or no}
              error := TRUE;
          {END IF}
      {END IF}

      IF error THEN
          WriteLn('DATA ERROR - reply not input as either yes or no')
      ELSE
          WriteLn('before you go out today take your ', garment);
      {END IF}
END. {weather}
```

```
what is the temperature outside today? 25
is it raining outside? answer yes or no yes
before you go out today take your  umbrella

what is the temperature outside today? 25
is it raining outside? answer yes or no don't know
DATA ERROR - reply not input as either yes or no
```

3.5 Boolean expressions

From the discussion so far it should be clear to the reader that Boolean expressions can only equate to one of two values, either TRUE or FALSE. Examples of Boolean expressions given so far have been (temperature < 15), (reply = 'yes'), (reply = 'no') and error.

The next example is a program that will input the name of a person and decide whether they are a suspect to a crime. It has been reported that the crime was committed by a person aged between 20 and 25 years, and between 66 to 70 inches tall. The program displays the name of the suspect if they fit this description.

```
PROGRAM suspect(INPUT, OUTPUT);
{
program to display the name of a suspect to a crime who is aged between 20 and 25 years and
between 66 inches and 70 inches tall
}
VAR
    name     : STRING;
    age      : INTEGER;
    height   : INTEGER;
BEGIN
    Write('Input name of suspect '); ReadLn(name);
    Write('age? '); ReadLn(age);
    Write('height? '); ReadLn(height);

    IF (age >= 20) AND (age <= 25) THEN
        IF (height >= 66) AND (height <= 70) THEN
            WriteLn(name, ' is a suspect and should be held for interrogation');
        {END IF}
    {END IF}

END. {suspect}
```

```
input name of suspect Artful Dodger
age? 23
height? 69
Artful Dodger is a suspect and should be held for interrogation
```

The conditions used in this program are (age >=20), (age <= 25), (height >= 66) and (height <= 70). It has been possible to combine these conditions into (age >= 20) AND (age <= 25), and (height >= 66) AND (height <= 70) by using the Boolean operator AND. A truth table for AND is given in figure 3.3. This table can be interpreted as follows.

If the (age >= 20) is condition X and (age <= 25) is condition Y, then X AND Y can only be TRUE if both condition X is TRUE AND condition Y is TRUE. In other words both conditions (age >= 20) AND (age <=25) must be TRUE for the expression to be TRUE. Therefore, if either condition X or condition Y or both, happen to be FALSE the complete expression given by X AND Y is FALSE.

Similarly both conditions in the Boolean expression (height >= 66) AND (height <= 70) must be TRUE for the condition to be TRUE. If either one condition or both conditions are FALSE then the Boolean expression is FALSE.

In the program, if the age is between 20 and 25 years, then the computer executes the next if statement, and if the height is between 66 and 70 inches then the name of the suspect is printed.

This program can be reconstructed, by omitting the second if..then statement, and combining the Boolean conditions for age and height as follows.

condition X	condition Y	X AND Y
FALSE	FALSE	FALSE
FALSE	TRUE	FALSE
TRUE	FALSE	FALSE
TRUE	TRUE	TRUE

figure 3.3 truth table for logical AND

```
IF (age >= 20) AND (age <= 25) AND (height >= 66) AND (height <= 70) THEN
    WriteLn(name, ' is a suspect and should be held for interrogation');
{END IF}
```

The same program can be reconstructed yet again using different Boolean conditions and the logical operator OR. By considering the age and height to lie outside the ranges it is possible to construct the following Boolean expressions:

$$(age < 20) \text{ OR } (age > 25)$$
$$(height < 66) \text{ OR } (height > 70)$$

From the truth table for logical OR, given in figure 3.4, if (age < 20) is condition X, and (age > 25) is condition Y, then X OR Y is TRUE if X is TRUE, or Y is TRUE, or both are TRUE.

Similarly, if (height < 66) is condition X, and (height > 70) is condition Y, then X OR Y is TRUE if X is TRUE, or Y is TRUE, or both are TRUE.

The conditions for age and height can also be combined into (age < 20) OR (age > 25) OR (height < 66) OR (height > 70).

Thus if any one of the conditions is TRUE the entire Boolean expression is TRUE, and the suspect is released. However, if all the conditions are FALSE, then the entire Boolean expression must be FALSE, the suspect is between 20 and 25 years of age and between 66 and 70 inches tall, and is held for further interrogation, as depicted in the next program.

Boolean expressions and variables can have their values changed by using the NOT operator. If the Boolean variable *error* was TRUE, then *NOT error* would be FALSE. Similarly if *error* was FALSE then *NOT error* would be TRUE.

condition X	condition Y	X OR Y
FALSE	FALSE	FALSE
FALSE	TRUE	TRUE
TRUE	FALSE	TRUE
TRUE	TRUE	TRUE

figure 3.4 truth table for logical OR

```
PROGRAM suspect(INPUT, OUTPUT);
{
program to display the name of a suspect to a crime who is aged between 20 and 25 years and
between 66 inches and 70 inches tall
}
VAR
    name    : STRING;
    age     : INTEGER;
    height  : INTEGER;
BEGIN
    Write('Input name of suspect '); ReadLn(name);
    Write('age? '); ReadLn(age);
    Write('height? '); ReadLn(height);
    IF (age < 20) OR (age > 25) OR (height < 66) OR (height > 70) THEN
        WriteLn(name, ' is not a suspect and should be released')
    ELSE
        WriteLn(name, ' is a suspect and should be held for interrogation');
    {END IF}
END. {suspect}
```

```
input name of suspect Bill Sykes
age? 44
height? 68
Bill Sykes is not a suspect and should be released

input name of suspect Artful Dodger
age? 23
height? 69
Artful Dodger is a suspect and should be held for interrogation
```

3.6 Case

An ordinal type has a value that belongs to an ordered set of items. For example integers are ordinal types since they belong to the set of values from -32768 to +32767. A character is an ordinal type since it belongs to the ASCII character set of values from the *null* character to the *del* character. Real numbers and strings are **not** ordinal types.

If selection is to be based upon an ordinal type then a CASE statement can be used in preference to if..then..else statements.

The syntax of the case statement is given in figure 3.5. The expression must evaluate to an ordinal value. Each possible ordinal value is represented as a case label, which indicates the statement to be executed corresponding to the value of the expression. Those values that are not represented by case labels will result in the statement after ELSE being executed.

In the example that follows a user is invited to input a value for a motorway junction on the M2 in

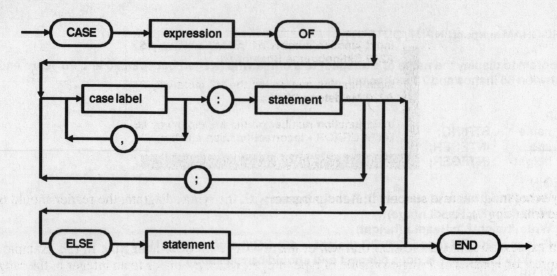

figure 3.5 syntax diagram for a CASE statement

Kent. Depending upon the value of the junction from 1 to 7, the destination of the adjoining roads at that junction are displayed. If the value input is not in the range 1..7 the statement after the ELSE will warn the user of the data error. After the appropriate statement has been executed the computer branches to the END of the case statement.

```
PROGRAM motorway(INPUT, OUTPUT);
{
program to demonstrate the use of the CASE statement
}
VAR
   junction : INTEGER;
BEGIN
   Write('input junction number on the M2 motorway ');
   ReadLn(junction);

   CASE junction OF
   1 : WriteLn('A2 only');
   2 : WriteLn('A228 Snodland Rochester');
   3 : WriteLn('A229 Maidstone Chatham');
   4 : WriteLn('A278 Gillingham');
   5 : WriteLn('A249 Sittingbourne Sheerness');
   6 : WriteLn('A251 Ashford Faversham');
   7 : WriteLn('A2 Canterbury Dover/ A299 Margate Ramsgate');
   ELSE
      WriteLn('DATA ERROR - incorrect junction number');
   END; {CASE}
END. {motorway}
```

```
input junction number on the M2 motorway 5
A249 Sittingbourne Sheerness

input junction number on the M2 motorway 3
A229 Maidstone Chatham

input junction number on the M2 motorway 66
DATA ERROR - incorrect junction number
```

By comparing the case statement in the program with the syntax diagram, the reader should note the following points.

An expression is any expression that will evaluate to an item of ordinal type. In this example the expression consists of a single variable of type integer, which evaluates to an integer in the range 1 .. 7.

A case label is any value that corresponds to the ordinal type in the expression. Case labels in this example represent the junction numbers 1, 2, 3, 4, 5, 6 and 7. Case labels must be unique.

The use of else is optional, and used for the purpose of trapping any values of the expression that are not represented as case labels.

The case statement terminates with the reserved word END.

3.7 Worked examples

This section contains two programs to further demonstrate the use of if..then..else and case statements.

The first program in this section validates a date in the twentieth century. It checks that the number of months in a year cannot exceed 12, and that the number of days in each month has not been exceeded. The program also reports on Leap Years.

Notice the use of the Boolean variable **error** to trap a possible error in the value for months.

The syntax of the if..then..else statement, would suggest that only a single statement can be used after THEN and after ELSE. What if several statements are to be executed in response to a

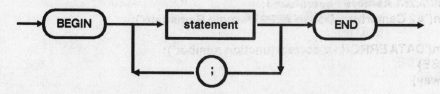

figure 3.6 syntax of a compound statement

condition being either true or false, how does the syntax cope with such a situation? Well the syntax cannot be changed, however, the statement can be a compound statement that contains as many statements as necessary. Figure 3.6 illustrates the syntax of a compound statement. The use of a compund statement is given in the if..then..else statement used to test for a Leap Year.

Notice from the program that if a year is a Leap Year then the statements bracketed between the BEGIN .. END of the compound statement will be executed. Notice that it would be wrong to put a semicolon at the after the END of the compound statement since this would split the if..then..else statement into two statements, which would result in a syntax error.

The method of determining a Leap Year has been to divide the year by 4, and testing for no remainder. For example, if the year is 1992, then 1992 MOD 4 is 498 after division with a remainder 0. Therefore the condition (1992 MOD 4 = 0) would be TRUE for a Leap Year. Clearly if the year was 1993, then 1993 MOD 4 is 498 after division with a remainder 1. Therefore the condition (1993 MOD 4 = 0) would be FALSE for a non Leap Year.

```
PROGRAM validate(INPUT, OUTPUT);
{
program to validate a date in the format dd mm yy
}
VAR
    day, month, year   : INTEGER;
    NumberOfdays       : INTEGER;
    error              : BOOLEAN;
BEGIN
    WriteLn('input a date in the twentieth century');
    Write('day '); ReadLn(day);
    Write('month '); ReadLn(month);
    Write('year '); ReadLn(year);

    error := FALSE;

    {calculate number of days in a month and check for Leap Year}
    CASE month OF
    1,3,5,7,8,10,12 :  NumberOfDays := 31;
    4,6,9,11        :  NumberOfDays := 30;
    2               :  IF year MOD 4 = 0 THEN
                       BEGIN
                           NumberOfDays := 29;
                           WriteLn(year:4, ' is a Leap Year');
                       END
                       ELSE
                           NumberOfDays := 28;
                       {END IF}
    ELSE
    error := TRUE;
    END; {CASE}
```

50

```
    IF (day > NumberOfDays) OR error THEN
        WriteLn('DATA ERROR - check day or month')
    ELSE
        WriteLn('date checked and is valid');
    {END IF}
END. {validate}
```

```
input a date in the twentieth century
day 18
month 3
year 1987
date checked and is valid

input a date in the twentieth century
day 12
month 2
year 1992
1992 is a Leap Year
date checked and is valid

input a date in the twentieth century
day 30
month 2
year 1987
DATA ERROR - check day or month
```

In the final example of this chapter, a program is written to mimic a simple calculator. The user is invited to type the value of two integers, and to state whether the integers are to be added (+), subtracted (-), multiplied (*) or divided (/).

A case statement is used to select the appropriate calculation corresponding to the arithmetic operator that was input. Since the result of a division by zero will give a meaningless answer, the program includes an if..then..else statement to trap a zero divisor.

```
PROGRAM calculator (INPUT, OUTPUT);
{
program to add, subtract, multiply or divide two numbers
}
VAR
    first, second   : INTEGER;
    result          : REAL;
    operator        : CHAR;
    error           : BOOLEAN;
```

51

```
BEGIN
    Write('input first number ');      ReadLn(first);
    Write('input second number ');ReadLn(second);
    Write('input operator ');          ReadLn(operator);

    error:=FALSE;

    CASE operator OF
    '+'    : result:=first+second;
    '-'    : result:=first-second;
    '*'    : result:=first*second;
    '/'    : BEGIN
             IF second = 0 THEN
                 error := TRUE
             ELSE
                 result:=first/second;
             {END IF}
         END
    ELSE
        error := TRUE;
    END; {CASE}

    IF error THEN
        WriteLn('DATA ERROR - illegal operator or attempt to divide by zero')
    ELSE
        WriteLn('=',result:8:0);
    {END IF}
END. {calculator}
```

Note sssss in this specimen output denotes spaces generated by the format result:8:0 in the WriteLn statement.

```
input first number 250
input second number 75
input operator +
= sssss325

input first number 18
input second number 26
input operator *
= sssss468

input first number 35
input second number 0
input operator /
DATA ERROR - illegal operator or attempt to divide by zero

input first number 121
input second number 11
input operator x
DATA ERROR - illegal operator or attempt to divide by zero
```

3.8 Summary

● A Boolean expression or variable of Boolean type equates to either TRUE or FALSE.

● Depending upon the result of the Boolean expression or variable it is possible for the computer to select different statements in an **if** statement.

● Boolean variables can be used in place of a Boolean expression in an **if** statement.

● Boolean expressions and Boolean variables can be combined into one Boolean expression by using the Boolean operators AND and OR.

● **If** statements may be nested, one within another.

● In general, an **else** is associated with the closest **if** not already associated with an **else**.

● When more than one statement is to be executed after THEN, ELSE or a case label, the statements must be represented as a compound statement bracketed by the words BEGIN and END.

● When selection is based upon an ordinal type, a **case** statement may be used.

● All case labels must be unique and of an ordinal type compatible with the selector type.

3.9 Questions

1. If A=1, B=-2, C=3, D=4, E='S' and F='J' then state whether the following conditions are true or false.

a. A=B   b. A>B   c. (A<C) AND (B<D) d. (A<C) AND (B>D) e. (A>B) OR (C<D)
f. E>F   g. ((A+C)>(B-D)) AND ((B+C)<(D-A))

2. How would you code the following conditions in Pascal?

a. X is equal to Y   b. X is not equal to Y   c. A is less than or equal to B
d. Q is not greater than T   e. X is greater than or equal to Y
f. X is less than or equal to Y and A is not equal to B
g. A is greater than 18 and H is greater than 68 and W is greater than 75
h. G is less than 100 and greater than 50
i. H is less than 50 or greater than 100.

3. Trace through the following segment of code for each new value of A,B and C, and state the output in each case.

a. A=16, B=16, C=32 b. A=16, B=-18, C=32   c. A=-2, B=-4, C=16

```
IF A>0 THEN
    IF B<0 THEN WriteLn('x')
    ELSE IF C>20 THEN  WriteLn('y')
ELSE
    WriteLn('z');
```

4. Modify the suspect program given in the chapter to cater for both sexes, and eliminate all women from the list of suspects.

5. A worker is paid at the hourly rate of £8 per hour for the first 35 hours worked. Thereafter overtime is paid at 1.5 times the hourly rate for the next 25 hours worked and 2 times the hourly rate for further hours worked. Write a program to input the number of hours worked per week, calculate and output the overtime paid.

6. A salesperson earns commission on the value of sales. The following table shows the scale of the commission. Write a program to input a figure for the value of sales, calculate and output the commission.

value of sales	% commission
£1 - £999	1
£1000 - £9999	5
£10000 - £99999	10

7. A barometer dial is calibrated into the following climatic conditions STORM RAIN CHANGE FAIR and VERY DRY. Write a program that will input one of these readings and output what to wear from the following rules.

STORM	wear overcoat and hat.
RAIN	wear raincoat and take umbrella.
CHANGE	behave as for FAIR if it rained yesterday and as for RAIN if it did not.
FAIR	wear jacket and take umbrella.
VERY DRY	wear jacket.

8. A bicycle shop in Oxford hires bicycles by the day at different rates throughout the year, according to the season. The proprietor also gives a discount on the number of days a bicycle is hired. If the hire period is greater than 7 days, then a reduction of 25% is made. For every bicycle hired a returnable deposit of £50 must be paid.

Write a program to input the season and the number of days hire, calculate and display the cost of the hire including the returnable deposit.

season	charge
Spring	£5.00
Summer	£7.50
Autumn	£3.75
Winter	£2.50

4.
Repeating statements

This chapter can be considered as a milestone within the book, since it brings together the work of the previous three chapters and shows how statements can be repeated under different conditions.

Contents

4.1 While..do

A while loop will allow a statement to be repeated zero or more times. The syntax of the while loop is given in figure 4.1, where expression is a Boolean expression and statement can be a single statement or a compound statement to be repeated.

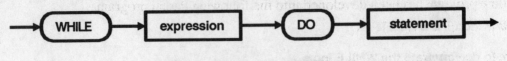

figure 4.1 syntax of a WHILE loop

Consider the use of a while loop to display numbers on a screen while the numbers are not zero.

A segment of the program follows.

```
ReadLn(number);
WHILE number < > 0 DO
BEGIN
    WriteLn(number:3);
    ReadLn(number);
END; {WHILE}
```

If the first number to be read is zero then the Boolean expression *number <> 0* will be FALSE. The computer will not enter the loop but branch to the next executable statement after the {WHILE} comment at end of the loop. Since the loop was not entered the contents of the loop is said to have been repeated zero times.

However, if the first number to be read was non-zero, the Boolean expression would be TRUE, and the computer would execute the statements contained within the loop. To this end the number would be written on the screen and the next number input at the keyboard. The computer then returns to the line containing the Boolean expression which is re-evaluated to test whether the new number is not zero. If the condition is TRUE the computer continues to execute the statements in the loop. If the condition is FALSE the computer will branch to the next executable statement after the {WHILE} comment that effectively marks the end of the loop.

Restating the behaviour of the while loop, if the first number read is zero then the loop is not entered, the statements within the loop have been repeated zero times. If the second number to be read is zero the statements in the loop will have been repeated once. If the third number to be read is zero the statements in the loop will have been repeated twice, etc. Therefore, if the hundredth number to be read is zero the statements inside the loop will have been repeated ninety-nine times.

Note - the BEGIN..END statements within the while loop represent the beginning and end of a compound statement. If there is more than one statement to be repeated it is mandatory that a compound statement is used.

Warning! The syntax of the while statement does NOT terminate with END. In the example the END belongs to the compound statement. A while loop that contained only ONE non-compound statement, would NOT contain an END.

The outline program has been developed into the following Pascal program.

```
PROGRAM loop(INPUT,OUTPUT);
{
program to demonstrate the WHILE loop
}
VAR
   value : INTEGER;
BEGIN
   Write('input an integer - terminate with 0 '); ReadLn(value);

   WHILE (value < > 0) DO
   BEGIN
      WriteLn(value:3);
      Write('input an integer - terminate with 0 '); ReadLn(value);
   END; {WHILE}
END. {loop}
```

The specimen outputs from the program shows (i) the statements within the loop being repeated twice, and (ii) the statements within the loop not being repeated at all.

```
input an integer - terminate with 0 36
36
input an integer - terminate with 0 18
18
input an integer - terminate with 0 0
```

```
input an integer - terminate with 0 0
```

The program suspect, taken from section 3.5 in the previous chapter, has been re-constructed to include a while loop to allow the program to be repeated many times without the need to re-run the program.

Before the while loop is entered the user is requested to input the name of a suspect. If the word END is input, the Boolean expression used to control the while loop, name < > 'END', will become FALSE, and the computer will branch to the statement after the {WHILE} comment that marks the end of the loop.

As long as END is not input in response to the prompt to input the name of a suspect, the computer will continue to process the details of all suspects to the crime.

```
PROGRAM suspect(INPUT, OUTPUT);
{
program to display the name of a suspect to a crime who is aged between 20 and 25 years and
between 66 inches and 70 inches tall
}
VAR
    name    : STRING;
    age     : INTEGER;
    height  : INTEGER;
BEGIN
    Write('input name of suspect - terminate with END '); ReadLn(name);

    WHILE (name <> 'END') DO
    BEGIN
        Write('age? ');        ReadLn(age);
        Write('height? ');     ReadLn(height);
        IF (age >= 20) AND (age <= 25) THEN
            IF (height >= 66) AND (height <= 70) THEN
                WriteLn(name, ' is a suspect and should be held for interrogation');
            {END IF}
        {END IF}
        Write('input name of suspect - terminate with END '); ReadLn(name);
    END; {WHILE}

END. {suspect}
```

```
input name of suspect - terminate with END Smith
age? 20
height? 68
Smith is a suspect and should be held for interrogation
input name of suspect - terminate with END Jones
age? 26
height? 68
input name of suspect - terminate with END Evans
age? 25
height? 69
Evans is a suspect and should be held for interrogation
input name of suspect - terminate with END END
```

4.2 Repeat..until

Unlike a while loop a repeat..until loop will permit the statements within the loop to be executed at least once by the computer. The syntax of the repeat..until loop is given in figure 4.2,

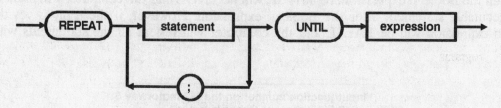

figure 4.2 syntax of a REPEAT loop

where statement refers to a single statement, which may be followed in sequence by other statements, and expression is a Boolean expression.

The program motorway, taken from section 3.6 in the previous chapter, has been re-constructed to include a repeat..until loop to allow the program to be repeated many times without the need to re-run the program. In this program the user is given the option to continue executing the statements in the loop until the reply to the question is no.

```
PROGRAM motorway(INPUT, OUTPUT);
{
program to demonstrate the use of the REPEAT .. UNTIL statement
}
VAR
    junction  : INTEGER;
    reply     : CHAR;
BEGIN
    REPEAT
        Write('input junction number on the M2 motorway ');
        ReadLn(junction);
        CASE junction OF
        1 : WriteLn('A2 only');
        2 : WriteLn('A228 Snodland Rochester');
        3 : WriteLn('A229 Maidstone Chatham');
        4 : WriteLn('A278 Gillingham');
        5 : WriteLn('A249 Sittingbourne Sheerness');
        6 : WriteLn('A251 Ashford Faversham');
        7 : WriteLn('A2 Canterbury Dover/ A299 Margate Ramsgate');
        ELSE
            WriteLn('DATA ERROR - incorrect junction number');
        END; {CASE}
        Write('continue? - answer [y]es or [n]o '); ReadLn(reply);
    UNTIL (reply = 'n');
END. {motorway}
```

Notice that the computer enters the loop without any test for entry being made. Hence the contents of a repeat..until loop will always be executed at least once. There can be many executable statements between the REPEAT and UNTIL reserved words. If the reply to continue is no then the Boolean expression, reply = 'n', will be TRUE and the computer will branch to the next executable statement after the Boolean expression. However, if the reply is yes then the Boolean expression will be FALSE and the computer will repeat all the statements within the loop.

```
input junction number on the M2 motorway 5
A249 Sittingbourne Sheerness
continue? - answer [y]es or [n]o y
input junction number on the M2 motorway 7
A2 Canterbury Dover/ A299 Margate Ramsgate
continue? - answer [y]es or [n]o y
input junction number on the M2 motorway 8
DATA ERROR - incorrect junction number
continue? - answer [y]es or [n]o y
input junction number on the M2 motorway 1
A2 only
continue? - answer [y]es or [n]o n
```

4.3 Input of numbers

Consider for a moment how the segment of code:

```
REPEAT
    ReadLn(x,y,z);
UNTIL z=0;
```

would read the following data that was input at a keyboard.

```
3  8  4  2  9 return
6  2  1  4  3  7 return
2  4  0 return
```

Note: a line of data is delimited by the return character.

In the first iteration of the loop $x=3$, $y=8$ and $z=4$. The three variables in the input list have been assigned data and the remainder of the data on that line is ignored. The next data to be read will be taken from the second line. In the second iteration $x=6$, $y=2$ and $z=1$. The remainder of the data on the second line is again ignored. Upon the completion of the third iteration $x=2$, $y=4$ and $z=0$. The iteration then terminates since the condition $z=0$ is now true.

The function of ReadLn, therefore, is to read data corresponding to the variables in the input list and then to skip to the next line, regardless of what data remains on that line.

The ReadLn statement can also be written without an input list. This implies that any data on the line is ignored and subsequent data to be read will be taken from the next line.

The ReadLn statement as the mnemonic suggests reads a line of data. The Pascal language also defines a Read statement, the syntax of which is identical to ReadLn. However, the semantics are quite different. Read has the effect of reading data regardless of how it is divided up into lines. The *return* becomes a data separator when reading numeric data. The segment of code:

```
REPEAT
    Read(p,q,r);
UNTIL r>10.0;
```

would read the following data that is input at the keyboard. Assume that the variables (p,q,r) are of type real.

16.3 7.9   8.1   12.9 *return*
8.7   3.2   9.5   7.4 *return*
11.6 *return*

In the first iteration p=16.3, q=7.9 and r=8.1. In the second iteration p=12.9, q=8.7 and r=3.2 (notice the *return* was used as a separator - its effect as an end of line marker was ignored). In the third iteration p=9.5, q=7.4 and r=11.6. Since the condition r>10.0 is now true, no further iterations of the loop are performed.

4.4 Input of characters

The statements ReadLn and Read can also be used for inputting characters, however, there is no requirement to separate character data by spaces. The following program illustrates how a sentence is input at the keyboard and the number of words in the sentence counted. It is assumed that only one space is used between words and the sentence is terminated by a full-stop.

```
PROGRAM WordsCount(INPUT, OUTPUT);
{
program to count the number of words in a sentence
}
CONST
    space = ' ';
    FullStop = '.';
VAR
    character       : CHAR;
    NumberOfWords  : INTEGER;
BEGIN
    NumberOfWords:=0;
    WriteLn('input a sentence on one line - terminate with a full stop');
```

```
    Read(character);
    WHILE character < > FullStop DO
    BEGIN
        IF character = space THEN
            NumberOfWords := NumberOfWords + 1;
        {END IF}
        Read(character);
    END; {WHILE}
    NumberOfWords := NumberOfWords + 1;
    WriteLn('number of words in sentence is ', NumberOfWords:3);
END. {WordsCount}
```

```
input a sentence on one line - terminate with a full stop
To be or not to be that is the question.
number of words in sentence is   10
```

In this last example the end of the sentence was detected by using the full- stop as a sentinel. However, it is possible to detect the end of a line of data by using the end of line function EOLN. The boolean function EOLN is true if the next character to be read is a return; otherwise, the value of the function is false.

How, you may ask, can the function be implemented for keyboard input, when clearly there is no way of knowing what the next character to be input will be?

The EOLN function for keyboard input in Turbo Pascal utilises a line buffer. As data are typed at the keyboard they are temporarily stored without being passed to the program. Only when the character *return* has been stored will the contents of the buffer be read, character by character, by the program. Since this is a complete line of data the EOLN function can detect when the next character is a return.

Figure 4.3 illustrates the use of a line buffer for storing and retrieving a line of characters. By using the concept of the line buffer it becomes clear why the output from the following segment of code appears as it does. The code reads characters from the line buffer and writes each character on a screen while the end of line character has not been read.

```
WHILE NOT EOLN DO
BEGIN
    Read(character);
    Write(character);
END;
ReadLn;
```

In running this program the reader might expect to input a character (with the system simultaneously displaying it on the screen) then write the character to the screen. This process is

The user types characters at a keyboard and they are stored in a line buffer

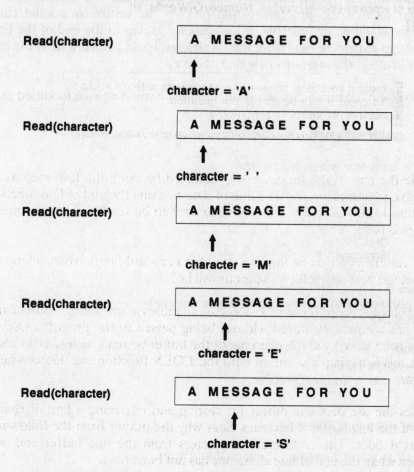

figure 4.3 an illustration of how characters are read from the line buffer

repeated until a return character is input. However, when the segment of code was run in a Turbo Pascal environment the output was as follows.

A MESSAGE FOR YOU
A MESSAGE FOR YOU

All characters are first input to the line buffer and simultaneously displayed on the screen (thus forming the first row of characters). The return character denotes the end of the line of input.

When the line of characters is complete (after return has been input) the program segment reads individual characters from the line buffer and writes each character to the screen (thus forming the second row of characters). When the next character to be read is return (character U will have just been written to the screen), the EOLN function is set to true and the computer will exit the while..do loop. However, the return character still remains in the line buffer. A further read statement in a later part of the program would pick-up the return as a valid character for processing. Since this would be undesirable, it is necessary to skip to the end of the line by using ReadLn and any further data to be read from the line buffer would be taken from the beginning of the buffer, which is in effect the start of a new line of data.

The last program to count the number of words in a sentence could now be modified using EOLN in place of the full-stop as a sentinal.

```
PROGRAM WordsCount(INPUT, OUTPUT);
{
program to count the number of words in a phrase
}
CONST
    space = ' ';
VAR
    character        : CHAR;
    NumberOfWords   : INTEGER;
BEGIN
    NumberOfWords := 0;
    WriteLn('input a phrase on one line - terminate with return key');
    WHILE NOT EOLN DO
    BEGIN
        Read(character);
        IF character = space THEN
            NumberOfWords := NumberOfWords + 1;
        {END IF}
    END; {WHILE}
    NumberOfWords := NumberOfWords + 1;
    ReadLn;
    WriteLn('number of words in phrase is ', NumberOfWords:3);
END. {WordsCount}
```

```
input a phrase on one line - terminate with return key
To be or not to be that is the question.
number of words in phrase is  10
```

4.5 Worked examples

In the first example of this section a program is to be written that will edit a single line of text. Within the input text will be found an opening parenthesis (, followed some characters later by a closing parenthesis). The text is to be output, with the characters between and including the parentheses removed. In this example you may assume that the character (always appears before the character), and both characters will always be present.

```
PROGRAM edit(INPUT, OUTPUT);
{
program to input a line of text, edit a portion of the text and output the editted text
}
VAR
   character : CHAR;
BEGIN
   WriteLn('input one line of text');

   {read and write characters up to ( }
   Read(character);
   WHILE character <> '(' DO
   BEGIN
      Write(character);
      Read(character);
   END; {WHILE}

   {read characters up to ) }
   WHILE character <> ')' DO
      Read(character);
   {END WHILE}

   {read and write characters as far as the end of the line}
   WHILE NOT EOLN DO
   BEGIN
      Read(character);
      Write(character);
   END;
END. {edit}
```

```
input one line of text
WriteLn('all the text between parenthesis should be suppressed');
WriteLn;
```

In the second example a program is written that will find and display the largest positive integer from a series of integers. The integers are input three to a line, over five lines. The maximum value of each integer on each line is displayed, then the largest integer from the fifteen integers is displayed.

```
PROGRAM BigOne(INPUT, OUTPUT);
{
program to input three positive integers per line and find and display the maximum value of the
integers from a single line;

the program is repeated for five lines of three numbers, and at the end of the program the largest
of the fifteen integers is displayed
}

VAR
    maximum    : INTEGER;
    largest    : INTEGER;
    x, y, z    : INTEGER;
    counter    : INTEGER;

BEGIN
    largest := 0;
    counter := 0;
    WriteLn('input fifteen positive integers');
    WriteLn('typing 3 numbers to a line over 5 lines');
    WriteLn;

    WHILE counter <> 5 DO
    BEGIN
        ReadLn(x,y,z);
        IF (x>y) AND (x>z) THEN
            maximum := x
        ELSE
            IF (y>z) AND (y>x) THEN
                maximum := y
            ELSE
                maximum := z;
            {END IF}
        {END IF}

        WriteLn('maximum value from this line is ',maximum:6);

        IF maximum > largest THEN
            largest := maximum;
        {END IF}

        counter := counter + 1;
    END; {WHILE}

    WriteLn('largest number in series is ', largest:6);

END. {BigOne}
```

```
input fifteen positive integers
typing 3 numbers to a line over 5 lines

34  56  98
maximum value from this line is    98
101  23  77
maximum value from this line is   101
52  7  88
maximum value from this line is    88
250  300  200
maximum value from this line is   300
16  17  18
maximum value from this line is    18
largest number in series is    300
```

4.6 Summary

● The statements within a while loop can be executed zero or more times.

● The statements within a repeat..until loop are executed at least once.

● Both loops use Boolean expressions to control the amount of repetition.

● In a while loop all statements within the loop will be executed while the Boolean expression is TRUE.

● In a repeat..until loop all the statements within the loop will be executed until the Boolean expression becomes TRUE.

● The function of a ReadLn is to read data corresponding to the variables in the corresponding input list, and then skip to the next line of input, regardless of what data remains on the line.

● ReadLn can be written without an input list if it is required to skip to the next line.

● Read has the effect of reading data regardless of how it is divided up into lines. Numbers must be separated by spaces or returns. Characters need not be delimited in this way.

● The EOLN function is used to detect the end of a line of input data.

● EOLN is TRUE if the next character to be read is return, otherwise the value of the function remains FALSE.

4.7 Questions

1. Write a program to display the message 'HELLO WORLD' ten times on the screen.

2. Write a program to input a message of your choice and the number of times you want to repeat it, then repeatedly display the message.

3. Return to your solution to question 4 in section 2.10 of chapter 2, and modify your program to output a table of values for temperatures in degrees Fahrenheit and the equivalent temperatures in degrees Centigrade. You should use a range of 32 degrees Fahrenheit through to 212 degrees Fahrenheit in steps of 10 degrees.

4. Write a program to output a table of conversion from miles to kilometres. The table should contain column headings for miles and kilometres. Miles should be output as integer values between 1 to 50, in steps of 1 mile, with a new headings being printed at the beginning of the table and after 20 and 40 miles respectively. Note 1 mile = 1.609344 Km

5. Write a program using REPEAT..UNTIL loops to output:

    a. The odd integers in the range 1 to 29.

    b. The squares of even integers in the range 2 to 20.

    c. The sum of the squares of the odd integers between 1 to 13 inclusive.

    d. the alphabet, both upper and lower case. Hint - use the CHR function and the ASCII code for the letter A through Z and a through z.

6. Write a program to find and print the arithmetic mean of a list of positive numbers. The number of numbers is not known in advance. Terminate the procedure with zero.

7. Write a program to calculate and output the overtime pay for ten employees and the total overtime paid. Overtime is paid at £12.00 per hour for every hour worked over 40 hours per week. Assume that employees do not work for fractional parts of an hour.

8. Write a program to input a phrase and display the ASCII code for each character of the phrase. Hint - use the ORD function.

9. Write a program to find and print the largest integer from ten integers input at the keyboard. Assume that numbers are input one per line.

10. Rewrite the program edit listed in section 4.5, so that it will output the contents of the parentheses only.

5.
Building blocks

By now the reader has enough information to write small programs.
At this stage it is important to explain how specific programming
activities can be formed into building blocks known as procedures.
The procedures can then be used as the basis for constructing
larger programs.

5.1 What is a procedure?

A procedure can be regarded as a group of self-contained declarations and executable statements that can be used to perform a particular activity. It is very important to stress the words self-contained, since a procedure can be written and tested in isolation from the final program. A procedure can be thought of as a building block. Different building blocks are written for different activities within a program. A complete program is built from many different building blocks or procedures, each having been tested, before being used as part of the whole program.

5.2 Where are procedures written?

Procedures are embedded into a program. They are written after the global constant and variable declarations of the program and before the executable statements of the main program. The position that procedures occupy in a program is depicted in figure 5.1.

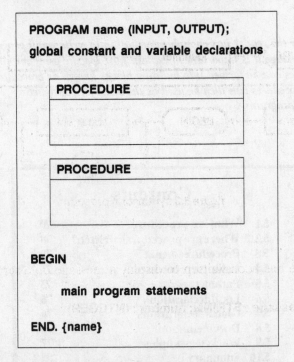

figure 5.1 procedures contained within a program

5.3 Procedure format

One of the rectangles that depicts a procedure, in figure 5.1, has been expanded to show the format of a procedure in figure 5.2.

The format of a procedure is basically the same as a program. A procedure must be given a name, which may be followed by a list of data declarations known as a formal parameter list. A procedure may contain a list of local constant and variable declarations.

The executable statements of a procedure are found between the reserved words BEGIN and END.

PROCEDURE name (formal parameter list);
local constant and variable declarations BEGIN   executable statements of procedure END; {procedure name}

figure 5.2 format of a procedure

The syntax diagram of a procedure is shown in figure 5.3.

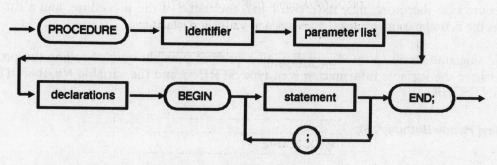

figure 5.3 syntax of a procedure

5.4 Calling a procedure

The following procedure has been written to display a message on a screen a specific number of times.

```
PROCEDURE display(message : STRING; number : INTEGER);
VAR
    counter : INTEGER;

BEGIN
    counter := 0;
    WHILE counter < > number DO
    BEGIN
        WriteLn(message);
        counter:=counter+1;
    END; {WHILE}
END; {display}
```

The first line of the procedure contains the name of the procedure, in this example display, followed by a list of data declarations known as the formal parameter list. In this example the

71

declarations are (**message : STRING; number : INTEGER**);

The formal parameter list has a dual role. In addition to specifying data declarations it informs the user about what data can be passed into the procedure, and what data can be passed out of the procedure. Remember a procedure is a self-contained mini-program, it should function where possible, independently of data that has been declared outside of the procedure. However, there may be a need to communicate with the procedure by calling it by name and passing data to it and/or receiving data from it.

To call the procedure display it is necessary to

(i) state the name of the procedure, and

(ii) state two items of data that correspond with the two items in the formal parameter list.

A procedure call, therefore, may have two parts, the name of the procedure, and a list of data known as the actual parameter list.

The following statements, printed in italics, all represent possible ways of calling the procedure display, where the variable **information** is of type STRING and the variable **NumberOfTimes** is of type INTEGER.

```
BEGIN
    display('Happy Birthday', 5);
END.


BEGIN
    information:='Happy Birthday';
    display(information, 5);
END.


BEGIN
    NumberOfTimes := 5;
    display('Happy Birthday', NumberOfTimes);
END.


BEGIN
    information:='Happy Birthday';
    NumberOfTimes:=5;
    display(information, NumberOfTimes);
END.
```

The following points must be observed when calling a procedure.

The list of constants or variables after the procedure name is known as the actual parameter list.

The number of actual parameters MUST be the same as the number of corresponding formal parameters.

The order of the actual parameters and the formal parameters MUST be the same.

The data types of the corresponding actual and formal parameters MUST be the same.

Having executed a procedure the computer returns to the next executable statement after the procedure call.

5.5 Parameters

The syntax of the formal parameter list is given in figure 5.4.

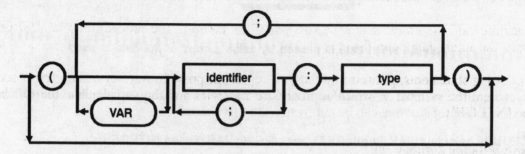

figure 5.4 syntax of a formal parameter list

By tracing through the syntax diagram the reader may notice that it is possible to represent four different formats of a formal parameter list.

(i) No formal parameter list - the declarations between the parentheses are by-passed.

(ii) A formal parameter list that contains data declarations NOT preceded by the word VAR.

(iii) A formal parameter list that contains declarations that are proceeded by the word VAR.

(iv) A mixture of declarations, those preceded by VAR and those not preceded by VAR.

In the example, the procedure display has a formal parameter list that fits the second category - (message : STRING; number : INTEGER);

The parameters *message* and *number* are known as **value** parameters. The data is passed to the parameters in this procedure by making a copy of the actual parameter data available to the procedure.

Figure 5.5 illustrates this fact.

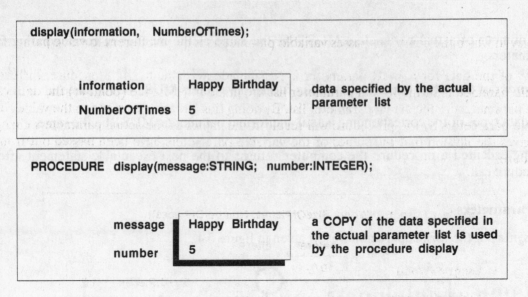

figure 5.5 when data is passed by value a copy of the data is used

Consider another example in which a procedure has been written to calculate the number of pieces of wood of set size that can be cut from a length of wood.

```
PROCEDURE calculate(VAR length:REAL; size:REAL; VAR pieces:INTEGER);
BEGIN
   pieces:=0;
   WHILE length >= size DO
   BEGIN
      length:=length-size;
      pieces:=pieces+1;
   END;
END; {calculate}
```

In the example, the procedure calculate has a formal parameter list that fits the fourth category - (**VAR length:REAL; size:REAL; VAR pieces:INTEGER**);

The parameters *length* and *pieces* are known as **variable** parameters, since they are preceded by the word VAR. The parameter *size* is a **value** parameter.

Variable (VAR) parameters are used if data is to be passed out from a procedure, or both into and out from a procedure. In this example *pieces* is a parameter that will pass the number of pieces cut from the length of wood, out from the procedure, since it is a result from a calculation. The parameter *length*, however, is a variable parameter that has passed into the procedure the length of wood, and will pass out from the procedure the amount of wood that has been wasted after the cutting has taken place. The variable parameter *length* can be thought of as an in/out parameter.

The way in which the computer passes variable parameters is quite different to value parameters.

A copy of the data for a VAR parameter is NOT made available to the procedure. Instead the variable parameters in the formal parameter list are made to reference (point at) the data values of the parameters in the actual parameter list. By doing this any changes made to the values of the variable parameters by the procedure will result in the values of the actual parameters changing. This gives the illusion that the values of the variable parameters have been passed out from the procedure.

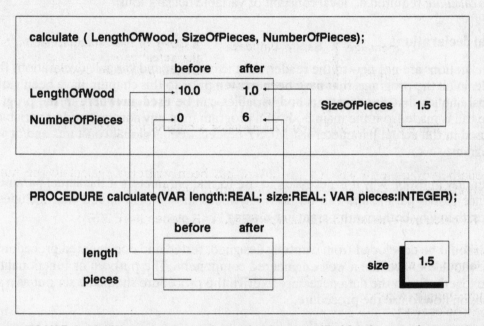

figure 5.6 VAR (variable) parameters point to the data specified by the actual parameter list

Figure 5.6 illustrates how the values of the variable parameters and the value parameter are passed for the procedure calculate.

If on a first reading of this section the reader finds the subject difficult, then remember the following points when constructing a formal parameter list of a procedure.

A VAR parameter is used whenever an item of data is passed out from a procedure.

If a parameter is only to be passed into a procedure then it does NOT require to be preceded by the word VAR.

5.6 Local declarations

In figure 5.2, the statement after the formal parameter list, indicates that local constant and variable declarations are made before the executable statements of a procedure are written. These represent the constants and variables that are local ONLY to that procedure. The constants and variables declared here CANNOT be used outside of the procedure. Remember that a procedure should be viewed as a self-contained unit that contains its own constants and variables.

In the procedure *display* the only local variable was a counter of type INTEGER, and the procedure *calculate* required no local constant or variable declarations.

5.7 Global declarations

Global declarations are not new to the reader. All the constant and variable declarations that have been made, in all the programs that have been written prior to this chapter, have been global. The word global implies that the constants and variables can be used anywhere in the program. If a procedure call is made from the main body of a program then any constant and/or variable names that are used in the actual parameter list MUST be declared as global constants and/or variables in the program.

The reader may question why it is necessary to use formal parameters if the actual parameters are global. Since global parameters can be used anywhere in a program, and that includes all the procedures, then why bother with parameter passing?

Programs should be developed from carefully designed, tested and documented procedures. Each procedure should behave like a well engineered component. The purpose or functionality of the procedure together with the data necessary to drive the procedure should be set out as a series of instructions on how to use the procedure.

In the development of a program that abandons the use of parameter passing, the developer would need to read through a procedure to distinguish between the local and global data in order to declare the global data. This in itself implies that such a procedure could not be treated as an off-the-shelf component that could be plugged into a program. In the production of a large complex program the sheer overhead of trying to manage global data would lead to poorly documented, error- prone programs.

5.8 Documentation

Before coding any procedures, regardless of how trivial, the reader should adopt the habit of completing a Procedure Documentation Form, shown in figure 5.7. This document is an aid to helping the programmer understand about the purpose or functionality of the procedure, determine what parameters are required and whether they are passed by value or as variables, and define the local constants and variables of the procedure. Completing this document might seem a chore, and a far cry from cobbling together some code on the computer, but it is a necessary part of engineering a robust, reliable software component.

Procedure Documentation Form

Procedure name:

Description of purpose of procedure and parameters:

number of parameters			VAR	
parameter name	type	in	out	in/ out

Local variables and/or constants

description of variables and/or constants	identifier	type	max size

figure 5.7 layout of a procedure documentation form

5.9 Worked examples

This section contains four examples of the use of procedures. Two of the procedures have already been used in this chapter, and two are new to the reader.

Each of the examples will contain the following documentation.

(i) A description of the problem to be solved.

(ii) A completed Procedure Documentation Form for the procedure to be coded.

(iii) A test program, called *TestHarness*, used to compile and test the procedure. The procedure and procedure call are shown in bold typeface.

(iv) Specimen results from the TestHarness program being run.

The first example requires a procedure to display a message a specified number of times on a screen. The message and the number of times the message is to be repeated are both passed to the procedure as value parameters.

Procedure Documentation Form

Procedure name: display

Description of purpose of procedure and parameters:

To display a message a number of times on the screen.

number of parameters	2			VAR	
parameter name	type	in	out	in/ out	
message	string	✓			
number	integer	✓			

Local variables and/or constants

description of variables and/or constants	identifier	type	max size
a variable to count the number of times the message is displayed	counter	integer	32767

figure 5.8 procedure documentation form for procedure display

```
PROGRAM TestHarness(INPUT, OUTPUT);
VAR
    information      : STRING;
    NumberOfTimes    : INTEGER;
PROCEDURE display(message : STRING; number : INTEGER);
{
procedure to display a message a number of times on the screen
}
VAR
    counter : INTEGER;
```

```
BEGIN
   counter := 0;
   WHILE counter <> number DO
   BEGIN
      WriteLn(message);
      counter:=counter+1;
   END; {WHILE}
END; {display}
BEGIN
   Write('input message '); ReadLn(information);
   Write('repeat how many times? '); ReadLn(NumberOfTimes);
   display(information, NumberOfTimes);
END. {TestHarness}
```

```
input message Happy Birthday
repeat how many times? 5
Happy Birthday
Happy Birthday
Happy Birthday
Happy Birthday
Happy Birthday
```

The second example involves developing a procedure that will calculate a modulus-11 check digit for a four-digit number. It is common practice to provide account numbers (e.g bank accounts, building society accounts, etc) with a check-digit. This digit provides a means for the computer to check that the account number has been correctly entered into the computer and that the digits have not been transposed.

A modulus-11 check-digit, for a four-digit number, is calculated in the following way.

Using the account number 9118 as an example: multiply each digit by its associated weight, here we have the weights 5,4,3,2 and calculate the sum of the partial products.

$$(5 \times 9) + (4 \times 1) + (3 \times 1) + (2 \times 8) = 68$$

The sum 68 is then divided by 11 and the remainder 2 is then subtracted from 11, the result 9 is the check digit. The account number, including the check-digit as the last digit, becomes 91189. If the value of the check-digit is computed to be 10 this is replaced by the character X and a check-digit of 11 will be replaced by 0.

Procedure Documentation Form

Procedure name: convert

Description of purpose of procedure and parameters:

To calculate a modulus-11 check digit of a four-digit account number

number of parameters	2			VAR	
parameter name	type	in	out	in/ out	
number CheckDigit	integer integer	✓	✓		

Local variables and/or constants

description of variables and/or constants	identifier	type	max size
individual digits of four-digit number	d1	integer	9
	d2	integer	9
	d3	integer	9
	d4	integer	9
sum of products	sum	integer	32767

figure 5.9 procedure documentation form for procedure convert

```
PROGRAM TestHarness(INPUT, OUTPUT);

VAR
   AccountNumber    : INTEGER;
   CD               : INTEGER;

PROCEDURE convert(number : INTEGER; VAR CheckDigit : INTEGER);
{
procedure to calculate the check-digit of a four-figure number
}
VAR
   d1,d2,d3,d4    : INTEGER;
   sum            : INTEGER;
```

```
BEGIN
    {extract the four digits from number}
    d1:=number DIV 1000;
    d2:=(number MOD 1000) DIV 100;
    d3:=(number MOD 100) DIV 10;
    d4:=number MOD 10;
    {calculate the sum of the partial products}
    sum:=(5*d1) + (4*d2) + (3*d3) + (2*d4);
    CheckDigit := 11 - sum MOD 11;
END; {convert}
BEGIN
    Write('input a four-digit number '); ReadLn(AccountNumber);
    convert(AccountNumber, CD);
    Write('number with check digit ', AccountNumber:4);
    IF CD =10 THEN
        WriteLn('X')
    ELSE
        IF CD = 11 THEN
            WriteLn('0')
        ELSE
            WriteLn(CD);
        {END IF}
    {END IF}
END. {TestHarness}
```

The results from running the program three times follows.

```
input a four-digit number 3456
number with check digit 34568

input a four-digit number 1001
number with check digit 10014

input a four-digit number 1234
number with check digit 12343
```

The third example involves writing a procedure to find the price of food at the Greasy Spoon Cafe, see section 1.1 in chapter 1.

Procedure Documentation Form

Procedure name: FindPrice

Description of purpose of procedure and parameters:

To search for the price of items of food from a menu.

If the item is found then a Boolean variable success is set TRUE, otherwise it is set FALSE

number of parameters	3			VAR	
parameter name	type	in	out	in/ out
item	string	✓		
price	real		✓	
success	boolean		✓	

figure 5.10 procedure documentation form for procedure FindPrice

```
PROGRAM TestHarness(INPUT, OUTPUT);
VAR
    food   : STRING;
    cost   : REAL;
    found : BOOLEAN;

PROCEDURE FindPrice(item : STRING; VAR price : REAL; VAR success : BOOLEAN);
{
procedure to find the price of an item on a menu at the Greasy Spoon Cafe
if the item of food is found then success remains TRUE and the price of the
item is assigned, otherwise success is set to FALSE and the price is set to zero
}
BEGIN
    success:= TRUE;

    IF        item = 'fruit juice' THEN           price := 0.30
    ELSE IF  item = 'soup' THEN                   price := 0.50
    ELSE IF  item = 'cold meat salad' THEN        price := 2.50
    ELSE IF  item = 'sausages' THEN               price := 1.00
    ELSE IF  item = 'bacon & egg' THEN            price := 1.00
    ELSE IF  item = 'cod' THEN                    price := 1.50
    ELSE IF  item = 'plaice' THEN                 price := 2.00
    ELSE IF  item = 'chips' THEN                  price := 0.75
    ELSE IF  item = 'tea' THEN                    price := 0.25
```

82

```
    ELSE IF  item = 'coffee' THEN                    price := 0.35
    ELSE
    BEGIN
        success:=FALSE;
        price := 0;
    END;
    {END IF}
END; {FindPrice}

BEGIN
    Write('input name of food from menu '); ReadLn(food);
    FindPrice(food, cost, found);
    IF found THEN
        WriteLn('£', cost:4:2)
    ELSE
        WriteLn(food, ' not on menu');
    {END IF}
END. {TestHarness}
```

```
input name of food from menu bacon & egg
£1.00

input name of food from menu lamb chops
lamb chops not on menu

input name of food from menu chips
£0.75
```

In the fourth and final example of this section a procedure is written to calculate the number of pieces of wood that can be cut to a set size from a length of wood.

Procedure Documentation Form

Procedure name: calculate

Description of purpose of procedure and parameters:

To calculate the number of pieces that can be cut to a set size from a length of wood

number of parameters	3			VAR	
parameter name		type	In	out	In/ out
length		real			✓
pieces		integer		✓	
size		real	✓		

figure 5.11 procedure documentation form for procedure calculate

```
PROGRAM TestHarness(INPUT, OUTPUT);
VAR
    LengthOfWood    : REAL;
    SizeOfPieces    : REAL;
    NumberOfPieces  : INTEGER;

PROCEDURE calculate(VAR length:REAL; size:REAL; VAR pieces:INTEGER);
{
procedure to calculate the number of pieces of wood that can be cut to a set size from a length of
wood
}
BEGIN
    pieces:=0;
    WHILE length >= size DO
    BEGIN
        length:=length-size;
        pieces:=pieces+1;
    END;
END; {calculate}

BEGIN
    Write('what is the length of wood? '); ReadLn(LengthOfWood);
    Write('what size pieces do you want to cut? '); ReadLn(SizeOfPieces);
    calculate(LengthOfWood, SizeOfPieces, NumberOfPieces);
    WriteLn('number of pieces ',NumberOfPieces:3);
    WriteLn('size of off-cut ', LengthOfWood:5:2);
END. {TestHarness}
```

84

```
what is the length of wood? 10.0
what size pieces do you want to cut? 1.5
number of pieces   6
size of off-cut     1.00
```

5.10 Summary

● A procedure should be written as a self-contained unit that represents a single programmed activity.

● A procedure may contain parameters and local constants and variables.

● When a procedure is called it is possible to pass parameters into the procedure.

● Upon return from a procedure it is possible to pass parameters out from the procedure.

● After the execution of a procedure the computer returns to the next executable statement after the procedure call.

● A parameter that is passed into a procedure only, is known as a value parameter, and is implemented by a copy of the actual parameter being made available to the procedure.

● A parameter that is passed out from, or into and out from a procedure is known as a variable parameter, and is implemented by the variables of the procedure making reference to the variables of the actual parameter list.

● A parameter that is passed out from, or into and out from a procedure is preceded by the reserved word VAR. Parameters that are only passed into a procedure may not be preceded by the word VAR.

● The number and type of actual parameters MUST match the number and type of formal parameters.

● The names of the actual and formal parameters can be the same or different.

● Constants and variables, including formal parameters, that are declared within a procedure remain local to that procedure.

● Constants and variables, including actual parameters, that are declared as global declarations at the beginning of a program can be used anywhere within the program, including all the procedures in the program.

● A procedure cannot be compiled on its own, and needs to be embedded within a test program.

● The test program, also known as a test harness, can be used to fully test the procedure.

● Procedures should be developed as off-the-shelf components that come complete with instructions for use.

5.11 Questions

1. If the following variables are global:

```
VAR
   A,B,C : INTEGER;
   X,Y,Z : CHAR;
```

State the errors, if any, in the following procedure calls and procedure declarations.

	procedure call	procedure declaration
a.	alpha	alpha(d,e,f);
b.	beta(A,B,C)	beta;
c.	delta(18'*')	delta(VAR C:INTEGER; Z:CHAR);
d.	gamma(X,Y)	gamma(i,j,k:INTEGER);

2. Trace through the following procedure and determine the value of result after each of the following calls.

```
test('a', result); test('B', result); test('c', result);

PROCEDURE test(letter : CHAR; VAR capital : BOOLEAN);
BEGIN
   IF (ORD(letter) >=65) AND (ORD(letter) <=90) THEN
       capital:=TRUE
   ELSE
       capital:=FALSE;
END; {test}
```

3. Write and test a procedure to calculate the diameter, circumference and area of a circle. The input parameter is the radius, and the output parameters are the diameter, circumference and area; (diameter = 2 x radius; circumference = 2 x PI x radius; and area = PI x radius x radius where PI=3.14159).

4. Write and test a procedure to convert an octal digit (base 8) to a description of the digit, for example 0 zero, 1 one, 2 two ... 7 seven. The input parameter is an octal digit, and the output parameters are a variable of string type containing the description and a Boolean variable denoting success if the digit was correctly converted.

5. Write and test a procedure to analyse whether a character is a vowel or not. The input parameter is a letter of the alphabet, and the output parameter is a Boolean variable indicating success if a letter was a vowel.

6. Convert the program motorway in section 3.6 to a procedure containing the following formal parameter list - (JunctNo:INTEGER; VAR destination : STRING; VAR error : BOOLEAN). The procedure will accept and validate a junction number and return the destination at that junction and whether the junction number was valid.

6.
Larger programs

This chapter explores the technique of dividing a programming solution into several parts, where each part is dedicated to a particular activity. The pencil and paper solution is tested and then coded into procedures that together form a Pascal program. The chapter also focuses the reader's attention on the need to develop documentation as a solution evolves.

6.1 Why design programs?

A beginner to programming may question why it is necessary to design programs at all. Indeed some programmers produce rough and ready solutions at a keyboard and continue to amend their programs until eventually the program appears to do what was expected. This approach often works for small programs, however, this is NOT a recommended approach to writing larger programs for the following reasons.

The final code is probably not easy to follow since it was no more than cobbled together.

The documentation of variable names and specific items of code are probably non-existent.

The program may not have been broken down into logical activities and written as separate procedures.

There was probably no test plan for testing the program or procedures and indeed the program might easily fail. Remember that such programs are produced by continuous amendments until the program appears to work. This changing or tinkering with code often leads to unforeseen side effects that may not manifest themselves for quite some time.

Lastly, what of the programmer who is asked to modify the program at a later date? Without sufficient documentation such a task is normally preceded by tracing through the program in order to gain an insight into how the program functions. Since program maintenance accounts for a substantial proportion of programming budgets, clearly any improvement in programmer productivity must be a saving.

6.2 Pseudo-code

The simplest way of learning about the fundamental techniques of program design is to work through a problem.

A program is to be written that will allow a teacher to input examination marks at a keyboard, categorise the marks into one of four grades and after all examination marks have been entered into the computer, display a breakdown of the number of marks in each category of grade.

The grade distribution is shown in the following table.

mark range	grade
100-85	distinction
84-65	merit
64-40	pass
39-0	fail

The number of examination marks is not known in advance, therefore, it will be necessary to introduce a sentinel mark, say 999, to signify the end of the marks being input. This value of course, must not be processed.

As early as chapter 2, section 2.8, it was stressed that a simple order for processing data follows the sequence:

> input data
> process data
> output results

In this problem each grade category represents the number of marks that fall into a particular mark range. For example, five distinctions would imply that five examination marks were within the range 100% to 85%. Each grade category must be initialised to zero before it can be used to tally the number of marks in each grade category. The simple processing model given in section 2.8 must now be modified to cope with initialisation.

> initialisation
> input mark
> analyse mark
> output results

The input of data, is the input of a single mark, one per line, at a keyboard. Since each mark must be processed BEFORE the next mark can be input it will be necessary to introduce a loop into the processing model.

> initialisation
> input mark
> while mark not equal to sentinel do
>   analyse mark
>   input mark
> end while
> output results

After the first examination mark has been input it is compared with the sentinel value 999. If the mark is NOT 999 then it is processed. A new mark is input and its value compared with the sentinel. This sequence of input mark, compare with sentinel and process mark continues while the mark is not the sentinel value. When the sentinel is input the computer will output the values stored in the four grade categories.

This first level of program design, provides the reader with an overview of the program to be written, and will form the basis for the main or control program.

The next stage is to examine each operation in the sequence and attempt to write down what is required. At present this is a pencil-and-paper exercise, and no attempt should be made to code the computer program or go anywhere near the computer!

Since initialisation consists of setting the value of each category of grade to zero the operation initialisation can be refined into the following design.

Pseudo-code for the procedure initialisation.

set distinction to zero
set merit to zero
set pass to zero
set fail to zero

The next operation to consider is input data. The data takes the form of percentage marks with the exception of the sentinel value 999. Whenever, data is input every attempt should be made to ensure that the data passed on for processing is valid. In this example the design of the part of the operation to input data should ensure that only valid data in the range 0 - 100 is passed on for processing, with the exception of the sentinel value.

Pseudo-code for the procedure input mark.

repeat
    read mark
until mark in range or sentinel

The next operation to process each item of data, involves each mark being examined to see which range of marks it belongs to. When the appropriate range has been found the value of the grade category will be increased by one. For example if a mark was to be found in the range 85 to 100 then the value of distinction would be increased by one.

Pseudo-code for the procedure analyse mark.

if mark in range 85 to 100 then
    increase distinction by 1
else
    if mark in range 65 to 84 then
        increase merit by 1
    else
        if mark in range 40 to 64 then
            increase pass by 1
        else
            increase fail by 1
        {end if}
    {end if}
{end if}

Finally the operation to output results is refined. This involves writing the values of the four grade categories to a screen.

Pseudo-code for the procedure output results.

write headings 'grade' and 'frequency'
write sub-heading 'distinction' and value of distinction
write sub-heading 'merit' and value of merit
write sub-heading 'pass' and value of pass
write sub-heading 'fail' and value of fail

Notice that in designing the program, the structures if..then..else, repeat..until and while..do are used in the same context as though they were Pascal control statements in a program. However, at this stage there is no need for the statements to obey the syntax rules of statements in a Pascal program. The format of this design is to write statements in English and Pascal, as a pseudo-code, that express ideas on how to initialise values, input data, process data and output results. The introduction of the Pascal-look-alike control statements is to document how the sequence of statements are to be obeyed.

6.3 Test data and desk check

Having designed a solution to a programming problem using pseudo-code it is now possible to verify that the program is correct. Indeed there is little point in continuing beyond the design stage to coding and implementing a program if the design is fundamentally flawed.

In order to verify that the design represents a correct solution to a problem it is necessary to trace through the pseudo-code using suitable test data. When choosing test data the following points should be kept in mind.

The type and nature of the data is representative of the problem. Numerical data, where applicable, should be chosen for ease of calculation.

Data should be chosen to test all parts of the design.

Data is meaningful and within well defined ranges. However, this assumes that the design being tested will always use valid data. This is not always the case since some designs will be specifically written to trap bad data. In such circumstances the data must be chosen to cover all eventualities.

To initially test the design of the program to categorise marks by grades the following approach is taken, using the Design Desk Check Document shown in figure 6.1.

Write the chosen test data and expected results from this data on the Design Desk Check Document.

Trace through the overall design of the program by starting with the call to initialisation. The name initialisation and the associated data identifiers are written on the form together with any values that are assigned to the data identifiers. In this case all four data identifiers are set to zero.

The next call is to input mark. The name input mark is documented together with the data identifier mark. The statement read mark is interpreted by using the first item of test data and assigning this value to mark. The condition associated with the repeat..until loop is documented and tested, the outcome of the test [T]rue or [F]alse is documented on the form.

In tracing the design the next statement to be executed is the while..do loop in the main program. The name main program and the condition in the while loop are both documented on the form. The condition is evaluated and the outcome written on the form.

Design Desk Check Document   <u>1</u> OF <u>1</u>

Test data	Expected results	
100	distinction	1
101	merit	2
75	pass	2
65	fail	1
55		
45		
35		
999		

main program/ procedure	data identifier/ condition	value
initialisation	distinction	0
	merit	0
	pass	0
	fail	0
input mark	mark	100, 101, 75, 65, 55, 45, 35, 999
	0 <= mark <= 100 or 999	T, F, T, T, T, T, T, T
main program	mark <> 999	T, T, T, T, T, T, F
analyse mark	85 <= mark <= 100	T, F, F, F, F, F
	distinction	1
	65 <= mark <= 84	T, T, F, F, F
	merit	1, 2
	40 <= mark <= 64	T, T, F
	pass	1, 2
	mark < 40	T
	fail	1
output results	distinction	1
	merit	2
	pass	2
	fail	1

figure 6.1 results of trace through pseudo-code

Since the condition statement associated with the while..do loop is true, the next call is to analyse mark. The first condition in the series of tests is documented, and evaluated. Since this condition is true, the data identifier distinction is increased by 1 to the value 1.

The next statement to trace is input mark within the while loop of the main program. The next item of data from the test data list is tabulated and the condition associated with the repeat..until loop is evaluated. This value is false, therefore, another mark is read from the test data list. The condition is again evaluated, this time it is true, and the trace continues with testing the condition in the while loop in the main program.

The trace through the pseudo-code and the tabulation of data identifiers/ conditions and associated values continues until the sentinel value is read from the test data list. The final call is to output results. The four data identifiers and their respective current values are documented on the form. The desk check appears to give the same results as those expected results predicted earlier, and at this stage it appears that the basic logical design of the program might function correctly.

The pseudo-code and testing phase is a necessary and fundamental part in engineering the construction of a program. This phase is vital in establishing the following points.

(i) attempting to find a method of solving the problem;

(ii) verifying that the logical design for processing the data is correct;

(iii) determining which procedures are to be used in the program;

(iv) determining the order in which the procedures are called;

(v) identifying variables that are required in the procedures and main program.

6.4 Documenting procedures

Before any detailed coding is contemplated it is wise to establish what each procedure will do, and what parameters are necessary in order to process data. By examining the data identifiers recorded for each procedure on the Design Desk Check Document it is possible to determine

(i) which data identifiers represent parameters and which represent local variables, and

(ii) which of the parameters are VAR parameters.

In the procedure initialisation the four identifiers are VAR parameters since their values are initialised in the procedure, and are required in other parts of the program, see figure 6.2.

In the procedure to input a mark, the only identifier is a VAR parameter since its value is required in other parts of the program, see figure 6.3.

In the procedure to analyse a mark, the identifier mark is an (in) parameter since it supplies a value to the procedure. However, the remaining identifiers are all VAR parameters since their values are needed in other parts of the program, see figure 6.4

Finally the procedure to display the results only requires the values of the four grades, and for this reason can be treated as (in) parameters, see figure 6.5.

93

Procedure Documentation Form

Procedure name: initialisation

Description of purpose of procedure and parameters:

To set the four grade counters distinction, merit, pass and fail to zero

number of parameters	4		VAR		
parameter name	type	in	out	in/ out
distinction	integer		✓	
merit	integer		✓	
pass	integer		✓	
fail	integer		✓	

figure 6.2

Procedure Documentation Form

Procedure name: InputMark

Description of purpose of procedure and parameters:

To input a mark in the range 0 to 100 or a sentinel value 999.
The procedure will not accept marks that are outside the range, except for
the sentinel value.
If a mark is outside the range the procedure will request that the mark is
input again.

number of parameters	1		VAR		
parameter name	type	in	out	in/ out
mark	integer		✓	

figure 6.3

Procedure Documentation Form

Procedure name: analysis

Description of purpose of procedure and parameters:

To classify a mark as belonging to a particular grade.
The number of marks in that grade is then increased by 1.

number of parameters	5			VAR	
parameter name	type	in	out	in/ out
mark distinction merit pass fail	integer integer integer integer integer	✔	↓↓↓↓	

figure 6.4

Procedure Documentation Form

Procedure name: results

Description of purpose of procedure and parameters:

To display the number of distictions, merits, passes and failures.

number of parameters	4			VAR	
parameter name	type	in	out	in/ out
distinction merit pass fail	integer integer integer integer	↓↓↓↓		

figure 6.5

6.5 Coding procedures

Having completed these forms it is now possible to extract enough information to code the name, formal parameter list and comments about the purpose of each procedure.

Each procedure is then coded directly from the corresponding pseudo-code, and should be embedded within a test harness program so that it can be compiled and tested before being copied as a well-engineered, off-the- shelf software component into the final program.

The pseudo-code design has been listed prior to the coding of each procedure. The reader should inspect the one-to-one correspondence that exists between the statements in the pseudo-code and the statements in the procedure.

At this stage each procedure is compiled and tested within its own separate test harness.

> **Pseudo-code for the procedure initialise.**
>
> *set distinction to zero*
> *set merit to zero*
> *set pass to zero*
> *set fail to zero*

```
PROGRAM TestHarness(OUTPUT);
VAR
    distinction, merit, pass, fail : INTEGER;

PROCEDURE initialisation(VAR distinction, merit, pass, fail : INTEGER);
{
procedure to set each of the grade counters to zero
}
BEGIN
    distinction := 0;
    merit := 0;
    pass := 0;
    fail := 0;
END; {initialisation}

BEGIN
    initialisation(distinction, merit, pass, fail);
    Write(distinction:3, merit:3, pass:3, fail:3);
END. {TestHarness}
```

> **Pseudo-code for the procedure to input a mark.**
>
> *repeat*
> *   read mark*
> *until mark in range or sentinel*

```
PROGRAM TestHarness(INPUT, OUTPUT);
CONST
    sentinel = 999;
VAR
    mark : INTEGER;

PROCEDURE InputMark(VAR mark : INTEGER);
{
procedure to input a mark, and validate that it is either a percentage or a sentinel value
}
BEGIN
    REPEAT
        Write('Input a percentage mark - type 999 to stop ');
        ReadLn(mark);
    UNTIL ((mark >= 0) AND (mark <= 100)) OR (mark = sentinel);
END; {InputMark}

BEGIN
    REPEAT
        InputMark(mark);
        WriteLn(mark:3);
    UNTIL mark = sentinel;
END. {TestHarness}
```

Pseudo-code for the procedure analysis used to process the data.

```
if mark in range 85 to 100 then
    increase distinction by 1
else
    if mark in range 65 to 84 then
        increase merit by 1
    else
        if mark in range 40 to 64 then
            increase pass by 1
        else
            increase fail by 1
        {end if}
    {end if}
{end if}
```

```
PROGRAM TestHarness(INPUT, OUTPUT);
VAR
    D,M,P,F : INTEGER;

PROCEDURE analysis(mark : INTEGER; VAR distinction, merit, pass, fail : INTEGER);
{
Procedure to increase appropriate grade counter according to the value of the mark
}
```

```
BEGIN
   IF mark > = 85 THEN
      distinction:=distinction+1
   ELSE
      IF mark > = 65 THEN
         merit:=merit+1
      ELSE
         IF mark > = 40 THEN
            pass:=pass+1
         ELSE
            fail:=fail+1;
         {END IF}
      {END IF}
   {END IF}
END; {analysis}

BEGIN
   D:=0; M:=0; P:=0; F:=0;
   analysis(100, D,M,P,F);
   analysis(75, D,M,P,F);
   analysis(65, D,M,P,F);
   analysis(55, D,M,P,F);
   analysis(45, D,M,P,F);
   analysis(35, D,M,P,F);
   WriteLn(D:3,M:3,P:3,F:3);
END. {TestHarness}
```

Pseudo-code for the procedure to display the results on a screen.

write headings 'grade' and 'frequency'
write sub-heading 'distinction' and value of distinction
write sub-heading 'merit' and value of merit
write sub-heading 'pass' and value of pass
write sub-heading 'fail' and value of fail

```
PROGRAM TestHarness(OUTPUT);

PROCEDURE results(distinction, merit, pass, fail : INTEGER);
{
Procedure to display the number of marks that fall into each of the categories of grades.
}
BEGIN
   WriteLn('grade frequency');
   WriteLn('distinction ', distinction:2);
   WriteLn('merit ', merit:2);
   WriteLn('pass ', pass:2);
   WriteLn('fail ', fail:2);
END; {results}

BEGIN
   results(1, 2, 2, 1);
END. {TestHarness}
```

6.6 Coding the main program

At this stage in the development of the program it is possible to record on a data analysis form, see figure 6.6, a description of the actual parameters, their identifiers, types and sizes. The names of the actual parameters can be the same as the formal parameters. Regardless of whether the names are the same of not, each procedure will either have a copy of the actual parameter in the case of (in) parameters or reference to the actual parameter in the case of VAR parameters.

The first level program design forms the basis of the main or control program. Now the names and the actual parameters of the procedures have been defined, the main or control program can be coded.

DATA ANALYSIS FORM			
description	identifier	data type	size
grade counters distinction	distinction	INTEGER	<=32767
merit	merit	INTEGER	<=32767
pass	pass	INTEGER	<=32767
fail	fail	INTEGER	<=32767
examination mark	mark	INTEGER	<=32767

figure 6.6

Pseudo-code design of the main or control program.

initialisation
input mark
while mark not equal to sentinel do
    analyse mark
    input mark
end while
output results

```
PROGRAM grades(INPUT, OUTPUT);
CONST   sentinel = 999;
VAR     distinction, merit, pass, fail, mark : INTEGER;

{procedures are deliberately omitted at this stage}

BEGIN
    initialisation(distinction, merit, pass, fail);
    InputMark(mark);
    WHILE mark <> sentinel DO
    BEGIN
        analysis(mark, distinction, merit, pass, fail);
        InputMark(mark);
    END; {WHILE}
    results(distinction, merit, pass, fail);
END. {grades}
```

6.7 A complete program

A listing of the complete program follows. By using an editor it was possible to copy the compiled and tested procedures from their test harnesses directly into the final program. At this stage no attempt should be made to rewrite the procedures, otherwise typographical errors are likely to occur.

```
PROGRAM grades(INPUT, OUTPUT);
{
program to input a number of examination marks, and classify each mark into one of four grades.
At the end of the data the number of marks in each category of grade is displayed
}
CONST   sentinel = 999;
VAR      distinction, merit, pass, fail, mark : INTEGER;

PROCEDURE initialisation(VAR distinction, merit, pass, fail : INTEGER);
{
procedure to set each of the grade counters to zero
}
BEGIN
    distinction := 0;
    merit := 0;
    pass := 0;
    fail := 0;
END; {initialisation}

PROCEDURE InputMark(VAR mark : INTEGER);
{
procedure to input a mark, and validate that it is either a percentage or a sentinel value
}
BEGIN
    REPEAT
        Write('input a percentage mark - type 999 to stop ');
        ReadLn(mark);
    UNTIL ((mark >= 0) AND (mark <= 100)) OR (mark = sentinel);
END; {InputMark}

PROCEDURE analysis(mark : INTEGER; VAR distinction, merit, pass, fail : INTEGER);
{
Procedure to increase appropriate grade counter according to the value of the mark
}
BEGIN
    IF mark >= 85 THEN
        distinction:=distinction+1
    ELSE
        IF mark >= 65 THEN
            merit:=merit+1
        ELSE
            IF mark >= 40 THEN
                pass:=pass+1
```

```
        ELSE
            fail:=fail+1;
        {END IF}
    {END IF}
    {END IF}
END; {analysis}


PROCEDURE results(distinction, merit, pass, fail : INTEGER);
{
Procedure to display the number of marks that fall into each of the categories of grades.
}
BEGIN
    WriteLn;
    WriteLn('grade frequency');
    WriteLn('distinction ', distinction:2);
    WriteLn('merit ', merit:2);
    WriteLn('pass ', pass:2);
    WriteLn('fail ', fail:2);
END; {results}

{main control program}
BEGIN
    initialisation(distinction, merit, pass, fail);
    InputMark(mark);
    WHILE mark <> sentinel DO
    BEGIN
        analysis(mark, distinction, merit, pass, fail);
        InputMark(mark);
    END; {WHILE}
    results(distinction, merit, pass, fail);
END. {grades}
```

```
input a percentage mark - type 999 to stop 70
input a percentage mark - type 999 to stop 20
input a percentage mark - type 999 to stop 50
input a percentage mark - type 999 to stop 80
input a percentage mark - type 999 to stop 85
input a percentage mark - type 999 to stop 45
input a percentage mark - type 999 to stop 999

grade           frequency
distinction     1
merit           2
pass            2
fail            1
```

6.8 Summary

● Write a rough outline of how to solve the problem. This will be very brief and the first attempt at solving the problem. No detailed coding is expected at this stage. From this outline it is possible to state the initial procedures that can be used in the program.

● For each procedure derive an outline of the code required, and refine this code further until you reach a point when the code will form a 1-1 correspondence with statements in Pascal.

● Invent simple test data and predict the corresponding results. Use this test data to trace through design of the program and produce a table of values for the intended variables. At the end of this desk check compare the values of the intended variables with the anticipated results. The results of the desk check and the anticipated results should agree, if not there is probably a logical error in the design of the program.

● Document the purpose and nature of all identifiers in each procedure.

● Code each procedure and embed it into a test harness program so that it can be independently compiled and tested.

● Code the global declarations and the main control program to form a skeleton of the final program.

● Copy, using an editor, the procedures from the test harnesses into the final program. This way the number of transcription errors that can occur in the procedures is drastically reduced.

● Compile and if necessary edit and recompile the program in order to remove any errors, including syntax errors.

● Test the program using the same test data that was used for the desk check. Ensure that the results are consistent with those expected. Apply more stringent tests on the program using data that, where possible, will test the program to its limits.

6.9 Questions

Design, test and implement programs as answers to the following questions.

1. Write a program to input a line of text, one character at a time, into the line buffer, and analyse the frequency of occurrence of each vowel. You can re-use the procedure developed in question 5 of the previous chapter, to test whether a character is a vowel or not. If the character is a vowel, then write a second procedure to analyse which vowel it is and increase the frequency count for the vowel. When the end of line is encountered display the frequency of occurrence of each vowel.

The basic design for the program might be as follows.

```
initialise frequency count
while not end of line do
    read next character
    analyse whether character is a vowel
    if vowel then
        increase appropriate frequency count for vowel
    end if
end while
display frequency count for each vowel
```

2. A schoolteacher keeps the names and addresses of his pupils on record cards. Pupils travel to school from many different villages in the rural region. The schoolteacher wants to design a computer program to count those pupils in his class who fall into the following categories.

distance to school	category
0 to less than 1 mile	A
1 to less than 5 miles	B
5 to less than 10 miles	C
10 miles or further	D

The school teacher has for reference a map of the region, with three concentric circles drawn from the school as centre having radii representing 1 mile, 5 miles and 10 miles respectively. From a pupil's record card he knows the village where a pupil lives, therefore, the distance from the school in a straight line can be obtained from the map.

For a class of pupils the data input to the computer will be the number of pupils in the class followed by the distance each pupil lives from the school. When data input is complete the computer will output the number of pupils in each of the four categories.

The basic design for this program might be as follows.

```
initialise each category and pupil counter to zero
input class size
while pupil counter is not equal to class size do
    input distance
    analyse distance and update category value
    increase pupil counter by 1
end while
output values of categories
```

3. The lengths of four sides of a quadrilateral and one internal angle are input to a computer. Design a computer program to categorise the shape of the quadrilateral as a square, rhombus, rectangle, parallelogram or irregular quadrilateral.

The rules for determining the shape of the quadrilateral are given in the following table.

name	right angle?	all sides equal?	opposite sides equal?
square	true	true	true
rectangle	true	false	true
rhombus	false	true	true
parallelogram	false	false	true
irregular	-	false	false

The basic design for this program might be as follows.

```
repeat
    input angle and lengths of four sides
    analyse shape
    display name of shape
    request for more data
until no more data
```

4. A motor insurance company uses the criteria of age, type of car and accident record in the last five years as a basis for estimating the type of insurance policy to issue to its customers.

The following table shows how each of the criterion are applied in issuing a policy.

age < 25?	foreign car?	accident?	type of policy
false	false	false	10% comprehensive
false	false	true	10% comprehensive + £50 excess
false	true	false	15% comprehensive
false	true	true	15% comprehensive + £50 excess
true	false	false	15% comprehensive
true	false	true	7.5% third party only
true	true	false	20% comprehensive
true	true	true	decline to issue policy

From the table if false is represented by 0, and true by 1, with the first column age < 25? having a weight of 4, the second column foreign car? having a weight of 2, and the third column accident? having a weight of 1, then each combination of true and false can represent a number. For example, false true false would be (0x4) + (1x2) + (0x1) = 2, similarly true false true would be (1x4) + (0x2) + (1x1) = 5, etc. If the result of each calculation is known as a score, then the score can be used to look- up using a case statement, the type of policy to issue.

Design a computer program to input the age of the driver, whether the car is of foreign manufacture, whether the driver has had an accident in the last five years, and the estimated value of the car. Calculate the score based upon this information. Look up the type of policy to issue, and display the premium based upon a percentage of the estimated value of the car.

The basic design of the program might be as follows.

```
repeat
    input data and calculate score
    look up policy and premium percentage
    display type of policy and cost of premium
    request for more data
until no more data
```

5. A picture framer has a supply of picture mouldings of various lengths. he wants to cut from them as many 0.5m lengths as possible and where a 0.5m length cannot be cut he will cut 0.2m lengths. Design a program to input the length of a strip of moulding, and calculate and output the number of 0.5m, and 0.2m lengths and the amount of wasted moulding. Repeat the program for different lengths of moulding being input, and keep a running total of the number of 0.5m and 0.2m pieces and the cumulative length of wasted moulding. At the end of the data output the total number of 0.5m, 0.2m pieces and cumulative length of wasted moulding.

One of the procedures to calculate the number of pieces of wood cut to a set size has already been developed in chapter 5, section 5.9. This can be incorporated into the following design.

```
initialise totals for 0.5m, 0.2m lengths and waste
input length of moulding
while length not zero do
    calculate number of 0.5m lengths and waste
    update total for 0.5m lengths
    calculate number of 0.2m lengths and waste
    update total for 0.2m length
    update total waste
    display results for length of moulding
    input new length of moulding
end while
display results for all mouldings
```

6. Consider the following rules for calculating income tax in a country.

Personal allowances are £1200 for a single person and £2300 for a married man. A child allowance is £100 per child. Taxable income is the amount remaining after deducting the personal allowance and the total child allowance from the gross income. Income tax is calculated from taxable income according to the following table.

taxable income on	% rate of tax
first £1000	0
next £1000	20
next £2000	30
above £4000	40

If gross salary, personal status (married or single) and the number of children are input to a computer, design a program to calculate and display both the taxable income and the income tax.

Assume for the purposes of this problem that only married couples are entitled to a child allowance, and that married women are classified as single.

The design for this program might be as follows.

```
repeat
    input data
    calculate income tax
    display results
    request for more data
until no more data
```

7.
Data structures

In the previous chapter the reader was introduced to a fundamental approach to solving problems in a way that solutions could easily be coded into a computer language. It is now necessary to introduce methods for storing information that lead to simple and more effective solutions. The chapter introduces two structures for storing data, the one-dimensional array and the record.

Contents

7.1 For..do

For..do is another statement for controlling the number of times a sequence of statements is executed. In other words it ranks along-side the while..do and repeat..until statements. The for..do statement was deliberately not introduced in chapter 4, with the while..do and repeat..until statements since its use is more relevant to controlling the access to an array data structure.

In the following segments of code a while..do loop has been used to count from 1 to 10 and a repeat..until loop has been used to count from 10 to 0.

```
counter:=1;
WHILE counter <= 10 DO
BEGIN
    Write(counter:3);
    counter:=counter+1;
END; {WHILE}

counter:=10;
REPEAT
    Write(counter:3);
    counter:=counter-1;
UNTIL counter = 0;
```

From these examples the reader should observe that in using either a while..do loop or repeat..until loop for counting it is necessary to include the following stages in the code.

(i) Initialise a loop counter.

(ii) Increase or decrease the value of the counter each time the sequence of statements within the loop has been executed.

(iii) Test the value of the loop counter to determine whether to exit from the loop.

When using a for..do loop these stages are automatically taken care of by the for..do statement. To illustrate the point, the first for..loop is used to count from 1 to 10, and the second for..do loop to count from 10 to 0.

```
FOR counter:=1 TO 10 DO
    Write(counter:3);
{END FOR}
FOR counter:=10 DOWNTO 0 DO
    Write(counter:3);
{END FOR}
```

The format of the for..do statement can be expressed as

FOR variable := lower limit TO upper limit DO, when the value of lower limit is less than the value of upper limit.

The for..do statement in this format functions in the following way.

(i) The loop variable is automatically initialised to the value of the lower limit.

(ii) The value of the loop variable is then tested against the value of the upper limit. If the lower limit exceeds the upper limit the computer will exit from the loop and branch to the next executable statement after the body of the loop. If the lower limit is less than or equal to the value of the upper limit then the computer will execute the statements within the body of the loop.

(iii) After the last statement in the loop has been executed the loop variable is automatically increased by 1.

(iv) The computer branches back to stage (ii)

If the value of the lower limit is greater than the value of the upper limit then the format of the for..do statement changes to **FOR variable := lower limit DOWNTO upper limit DO.** There are two differences in the manner in which this format functions.

(i) The computer will exit from the loop when the lower limit is less than the upper limit.

(ii) The loop counter is decremented by 1.

The syntax of the for..do statement is given in figure 7.1. Notice that both the lower and upper limits can be expressions that must evaluate to an ordinal value. Remember integers and characters are ordinal values, real numbers and strings are not ordinal. In the context of this chapter the lower and upper limits will either be integer values, variables or arithmetic expressions that equate to integer values. The statement that follows the for..do statement can either be a single statement, or a compound statement. In either case it is good practice to terminate the end of the loop with the comment {END FOR} or END; {FOR} respectively, since this clearly indicates the boundary of the loop.

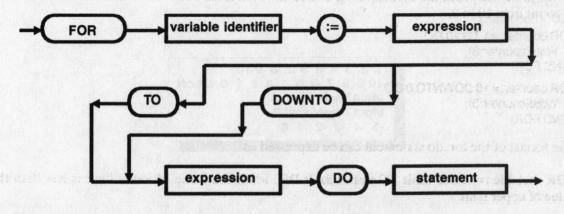

figure 7.1 syntax diagram of a FOR loop

The following example program shows how a for..do loop can be used to count from 1 to 10, 10 to 0 and between limits that the user inputs at run-time.

```
PROGRAM ForDemo(OUTPUT);
{
program to demonstrate the function of a FOR loop
}
VAR
    index            : INTEGER;
    lower, upper     : INTEGER;

BEGIN
    FOR index:=1 TO 10 DO
        Write(index:3);
    {END FOR}
    WriteLn;

    FOR index:=10 DOWNTO 0 DO
        Write(index:3);
    {END FOR}
    WriteLn(' lift off ');

    Write('input lower limit '); ReadLn(lower);
    Write('input upper limit '); ReadLn(upper);
    IF lower > upper THEN
    BEGIN
        FOR index:=lower DOWNTO upper DO
            Write(index:4);
        {END FOR}
    END
    ELSE
    BEGIN
        FOR index:=lower TO upper DO
            Write(index:4);
        {END FOR}
    END; {IF}
    WriteLn;
END. {ForDemo}
```

```
 1 2 3 4 5 6 7 8 9 10
10 9 8 7 6 5 4 3 2 1  0 lift off
input lower limit -5
input upper limit 0
-5 -4 -3 -2 -1 0
```

110

7.2 One-dimensional array

Consider for a moment how you would store, say, five integer values. The obvious answer would be to create five variable names:

```
VAR
    number_1, number_2, number_3, number_4, number_5 : INTEGER;
```

and assign a value to each consecutive variable.

```
number_1 := 54;
number_2 := 26;
number_3 := 99;
number-4 := -25;
number_5 := 13;
```

If the same approach was adopted to store, say, fifty integer values then the amount of coding would become tedious to perform. Clearly there must be a better way of storing data of the same type, so that the amount of coding can be reduced to a minimum.

Well there is, and the answer is to use an array. Arrays come in various dimensions, however, within the scope of this text only the one- dimensional array will be considered.

A picture of a one-dimensional array, containing five storage cells is illustrated in figure 7.2.

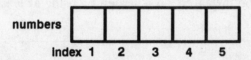

figure 7.2 the representation of a one-dimensional array

It is important to remember the following points.

(i) The contents of the array MUST be of the same data type. In other words an array can contain all integers, or all reals or all characters, or all strings, but not a mixture of each type.

(ii) Each item in the array is stored in a separate cell. If an array contained five integers, then each integer would occupy a single cell.

(iii) Each cell has a unique location value assigned to it showing its position within the array. This location value is known as either a subscript or an index.

(iv) The array is given only ONE name, irrespective of the number of items it contains.

(v) Before an array can be used it MUST be declared like any other variable.

The array depicted in figure 7.2 might be declared as follows.

VAR
   numbers : ARRAY[1..5] OF INTEGER;

This states that the name of the variable is *numbers*. It is an array containing five cells, having subscripts numbered 1 through to 5 respectively. The contents of the array is of type integer.

(vi) Access to an item of data within a cell is by using the name of the array followed by the position, subscript or index number, contained within square brackets.

To store the number 54 at cell position 1 in the array is possible by using the statement numbers[1]:=54; similarly to store number 26 at cell position 2 use numbers[2]:=26, etc.

7.3 Input and output of data

Figure 7.3 illustrates that the array called *numbers* contains five integers. These numbers can be stored in the array by direct assignment. For example the following five assignment statements would cause the numbers to be stored in the array as shown.

```
numbers[1]:=54;
numbers[2]:=26;
numbers[3]:=99;
numbers[4]:=-25;
numbers[5]:=13;
```

The contents of the array can be displayed on a screen by using at least one Write or WriteLn statement. For example,

```
WriteLn(numbers[1]:3);
WriteLn(numbers[2]:3);
WriteLn(numbers[3]:3);
WriteLn(numbers[4]:3);
WriteLn(numbers[5]:3);
```

would display the contents of the array on five lines of a screen.

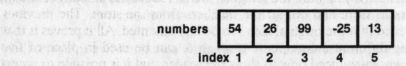

figure 7.3 the one-dimensional array containing integers

These statements have been incorporated into the following program so that the array *numbers* can be created and its contents displayed.

```
PROGRAM ArrayDemo(OUTPUT);
{
program to assign numbers directly to the cells of an array,
and display the contents of these cells
}
VAR
numbers : ARRAY[1..5] OF INTEGER;

BEGIN
    {direct assignment of numbers to cells of the array}
    numbers[1]: = 54;
    numbers[2]: = 26;
    numbers[3]: = 99;
    numbers[4]: = -25;
    numbers[5]: = 13;

    {the contents of the array can be displayed on a screen}
    WriteLn('contents of array');
    WriteLn;
    WriteLn('cell 1 ', numbers[1]:3);
    WriteLn('cell 2 ', numbers[2]:3);
    WriteLn('cell 3 ', numbers[3]:3);
    WriteLn('cell 4 ', numbers[4]:3);
    WriteLn('cell 5 ', numbers[5]:3);
END. {ArrayDemo}
```

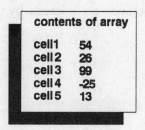

The original idea of introducing an array to store the integers, was to reduce the amount of coding required to assign the numbers to store and output the numbers from the store. The previous example hardly inspires confidence that the original idea can be implemented. All it proves is that the same name, *numbers*, using different subscripts, 1 through 5, can be used in place of five different names. The program was introduced only to show the reader that it is possible to access explicitly any cell in the array.

To reduce the amount of coding it is necessary to replace the explicit use of the subscript or index by a loop variable. Instead of explicitly coding numbers[1], numbers[2], numbers[3], numbers[4] and numbers[5] it is far easier to use numbers[index], and embed this statement in a for..do loop changing the value of index from 1 TO 5. For example numbers can be input and stored in the array using:

```
FOR index:=1 TO 5 DO
    Read(numbers[index]);
{END FOR}
```

and the contents of each cell of the array can be displayed using

```
FOR index:=1 TO 5 DO
    WriteLn(numbers[index]:3);
{END FOR}
```

This idea of using the loop variable, in this case index, to control access to the contents of the array is demonstrated in the next program.

```
PROGRAM ArrayDemo(INPUT, OUTPUT);
{
program to input numbers into a one-dimensional array and display the contents of the array
}
VAR
    numbers     : ARRAY[1..5] OF INTEGER;
    index       : INTEGER;

BEGIN
    {input numbers into the array}
    WriteLn('input five integers, one per line');

    FOR index:=1 TO 5 DO
    BEGIN
        Write('cell', index:2, ' ');
        Read(numbers[index]);
    END; {FOR}

    WriteLn;
    {output numbers from the array}

    WriteLn('contents of array');
    FOR index:=1 TO 5 DO
    BEGIN
        Write('cell', index:2, ' ');
        WriteLn(numbers[index]);
    END; {FOR}

END. {ArrayDemo}
```

114

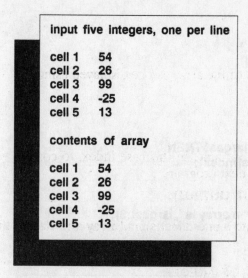

```
input five integers, one per line

cell 1    54
cell 2    26
cell 3    99
cell 4    -25
cell 5    13

contents of array

cell 1    54
cell 2    26
cell 3    99
cell 4    -25
cell 5    13
```

The use of a for..loop variable is not confined to the input and output of data from an array but can be used to compare data between cells. In this next program five numbers are stored in an array, the contents of the array is then inspected to find the largest number.

The for..loop variable index is used to gain access to consecutive items of data and compare each item with the largest number found so far.

```
largest:=numbers[1];
FOR index:=2 TO 5 DO
   IF numbers[index] > largest THEN
      largest:= numbers[index];
   {END IF}
{END FOR}
```

The variable largest is assigned the first value in the array. The loop variable is then set to access the remaining cells in the array. If a number in one of these cells is greater than the current value of the variable largest then largest is assigned this value.

```
PROGRAM ArrayDemo(INPUT, OUTPUT);
{
program to input numbers into a one-dimensional array and find and
display the largest number in the array
}
VAR
   numbers    : ARRAY[1..5] OF INTEGER;
   index      : INTEGER;
   largest    : INTEGER;
BEGIN
   {input numbers into the array}
   WriteLn('input five integers, one per line');
```

```
FOR index:=1 TO 5 DO
BEGIN
    Write('cell', index:2, ' ');
    Read(numbers[index]);
END; {FOR}

WriteLn;
largest:=numbers[1];

FOR index:=2 TO 5 DO
    IF numbers[index] > largest THEN
        largest := numbers[index];
    {END IF}
{END FOR}

WriteLn('largest number in array is ', largest:3);
END. {ArrayDemo}
```

```
input five integers, one per line

cell 1    54
cell 2    26
cell 3    99
cell 4    -25
cell 5    13

largest number in array is 99
```

7.4 Array of characters

A variable of string data type is represented as an array of characters, and the maximum size of this array in Turbo Pascal is 255 characters. In Turbo Pascal the size of the string is stored by the system as a character in cell 0 of the array. The length of the string can be obtained by taking the ordinal value of the character, for example in a string variable *characters* by ORD(characters[0]). The size of the array can therefore grow or shrink according to the number of characters that it contains. A declaration of an array of characters is not the same as the declaration of a string. The size of an array of characters is fixed at the time it is declared. For example

```
VAR
    alphabet : ARRAY[1..26] OF CHAR;
```

defines a fixed-length array that can accommodate 26 characters. Whereas the declaration

```
VAR
    characters : STRING;
```

defines a variable-length array that can accommodate up to 255 characters.

In Standard Pascal, an array of characters is NOT the same as a string. However, in Turbo Pascal this limitation is relaxed, and a variable defined as a string can be treated as a variable defined as an array of characters. Figure 7.4 illustrates an array that contains ten characters. In the program that follows, despite the data being defined as a variable of type string, it is possible to access each cell of this array to display the contents of the array.

characters	a	b	c	d	e	f	g	h	i	j
index	1	2	3	4	5	6	7	8	9	10

figure 7.4 a variable of string data type is stored as an array of characters

```
PROGRAM StringDemo(INPUT, OUTPUT);
{
program to demonstrate that a STRING data type is an array of characters
}
VAR
    characters  : STRING;
    index       : INTEGER;

BEGIN
    {input a string}
    Write('input ten characters ');
    ReadLn(characters);
    {output the contents of the string one character at a time}
    FOR index:= 1 TO 10 DO
        Write(characters[index]);
    {END FOR}
    WriteLn;
END. {StringDemo}
```

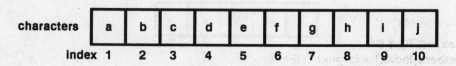

```
input ten characters abcdefghij
abcdefghij
```

In the next example a variable *word* is defined as data type string. Data is input and stored in the string. However, since the characters of the string will be stored in an array from cell 1 through to cell N, where N represents the length of the string, it is possible to inspect the contents of the array as though it was an array of characters. The length N of the string is automatically represented as a character in cell 0, hence ORD(word[0]) = N.

The purpose of the program is to test a word for being a palindrome, that is a word spelt the same backwards as forwards. The method used to test the word is to inspect the characters at either end of the word, if these are the same then the next two characters at either end of the word are compared. The comparisons continue until there is no match between characters, or there are no further comparisons possible. The movement of the indices is shown in figure 7.5.

117

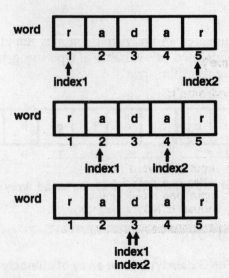

figure 7.5 stages in the comparison of characters,
where word[index1] = word[index2] in the program
that tests for a palindrome

```
PROGRAM palindrome(INPUT, OUTPUT);
{
program to input a word and test whether it is a palindrome
}
VAR
    word                : STRING;
    index1, index2      : INTEGER;
    CharactersMatch : BOOLEAN;

BEGIN
    {input word}
    Write('input one word ');
    ReadLn(word);

    {test for palindrome}
    index1:=1;
    index2:=ORD(word[0]);
    CharactersMatch:=TRUE;
    WHILE (index1 <= index2) AND CharactersMatch DO
        IF word[index1] = word[index2] THEN
        BEGIN
            index1:=index1+1;
            index2:=index2-1;
        END
        ELSE
            CharactersMatch:=FALSE;
        {END IF}
    {END WHILE}
```

118

```
{output result of test}
IF CharactersMatch THEN
    WriteLn(word, ' is a palindrome')
ELSE
    WriteLn(word, ' is NOT a palindrome');
{END IF}
END. {palindrome}
```

```
input one word radar
radar is a palindrome
input one word mouse
mouse is NOT a palindrome
```

7.5 Records

It was stated earlier in the chapter that the contents of an array MUST be of the same data type. In other words an array can contain all integers, or all reals, or all characters, or all strings, but not a mixture of each type.

This statement is perfectly true, however, it does not preclude a mixture of data types from being stored in the cell of an array provided that the types come under the umbrella of a record type.

A record is a collection of values, possibly of different types, whose components are accessed by name.

Figure 7.6 illustrates how a birthday date can be divided into the components day, month and year. Birthday is depicted as a record type, that contains the fields day, month and year, each of type integer.

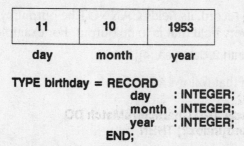

11	10	1953
day	month	year

```
TYPE birthday = RECORD
                    day    : INTEGER;
                    month  : INTEGER;
                    year   : INTEGER;
                END;
```

figure 7.6 the format of a record to represent a date

A user defined type declaration is a new concept in this book, however, it is a common practice when programming in Pascal.

The word TYPE is used once in a type declaration and must follow any constant declarations and appear before any variable declarations. The set order in a Pascal program or procedure is:

```
CONST
TYPE
VAR
```

The type of record that is used to represent a date of birth is defined as having a type called birthday:

```
TYPE
    birthday =  RECORD
                    day      : INTEGER;
                    month    : INTEGER;
                    year     : INTEGER;
                END;
```

A variable that is used to store the date of birth is then defined as:

```
VAR
    date : birthday;
```

This implies that the variable date contains three fields, day, month and year. To access each field it is necessary to qualify the variable date with the name of the field. For example

```
date.day:=11;
date.month:=10;
date.year:=1953;
```

would assign the day as 11, month as 10 and year as 1953, thereby representing a date of 11 10 1953. In the program on the next page, the values for day, month and year are input via a keyboard, hence the statement:

```
ReadLn(date.day, date.month, date.year);
```

Since the variable date is a record, its fields CANNOT be output by simply writing WriteLn(date). It is necessary to specify every field that is to be output. For example

```
WriteLn(date.day:2, date.month:2, date.year:4);
```

or as stated in the program that follows as:

```
WriteLn('day', date.day:2);
WriteLn('month', date.month:2);
WriteLn('year', date.year:4);
```

120

```
PROGRAM RecordDemo(INPUT, OUTPUT);
{
program to create a record and display its contents
}
TYPE
    birthday =   RECORD
                    day       : INTEGER;
                    month   : INTEGER;
                    year      : INTEGER;
                END;

VAR
    date : birthday;

BEGIN
    Write('Input a date of birth as DD MM 19YY ');
    ReadLn(date.day, date.month, date.year);
    WriteLn('day ', date.day:2);
    WriteLn('month ', date.month:2);
    WriteLn('year ', date.year:4);
END. {RecordDemo}
```

```
input date of birth as DD MM 19YY 11 10 1953
day 11
month 10
year 1953
```

The previous program can be extended to store more than one record. The variable name *date* needs to be changed and redefined as an array that will store records of type birthday:

dates : ARRAY [1..5] OF birthday;

	day	dates month	year
1	11	10	1953
2	18	03	1948
Index 3	14	06	1920
4	17	03	1960
5	25	09	1981

figure 7.7 array used to store records containing birthdays

Each record that is input at the keyboard can then be stored into consecutive locations of this five cell array, as depicted in figure 7.7. When all five records have been stored the contents of the array is then displayed on a screen.

```
PROGRAM RecordDemo(INPUT, OUTPUT);
{
program to create records, store them in an array and display the contents of the array
}
TYPE
    birthday =   RECORD
                    day      : INTEGER;
                    month    : INTEGER;
                    year     : INTEGER;
                 END;

VAR
    dates : ARRAY [1..5] OF birthday;
    index : INTEGER;
BEGIN
    WriteLn('input five dates of birth as DD MM 19YY, one per line');
    FOR index:=1 TO 5 DO
        ReadLn(dates[index].day, dates[index].month, dates[index].year);
    {END FOR}
    {output the contents of the array}
    FOR index:=1 TO 5 DO
        WriteLn(dates[index].day:3,dates[index].month:3,dates[index].year:5);
    {END FOR}
END. {RecordDemo}
```

```
input five dates of birth as DD MM 19YY, one per line

11 10 1953
18 03 1948
14 06 1920
17 03 1960
25 09 1981

11  10  1953
18   3  1948
14   6  1920
17   3  1960
25   9  1981
```

It is possible for a field of a record to also be of type record. For instance in figure 7.8 the record data type Names_Dates has two fields name and DOB. However, DOB has a data type birthday, where birthday has previously been defined as a record type. As figure 7.8 illustrates, a single field DOB of a record, can itself be a record containing the fields day, month and year.

name		DOB	
Jane	11	10	1953
	day	month	year

```
TYPE Names_Dates = RECORD
                       name : STRING;
                       DOB  : birthday;
                   END;
```

figure 7.8 the format of a record to represent a name and a date

The next program is merely an extension of the previous program. Instead of storing records containing dates of birth in an array it stores the names of people and their corresponding dates of birth in an array. Figure 7.9 illustrates the storage of the new records in the array.

		name	day	DOB month	year
	1	Jane	11	10	1953
	2	Fred	18	03	1948
index	3	Henry	14	06	1920
	4	Patrick	17	03	1960
	5	Susan	25	09	1981

figure 7.9 array used to store records containing names and birthdays

```
PROGRAM RecordDemo(INPUT, OUTPUT);
{
program to create records, store them in an array and display the contents of the array
}
TYPE
   birthday =  RECORD
                   day    : INTEGER;
                   month  : INTEGER;
                   year   : INTEGER;
               END;

   Names_Dates =  RECORD
                      name  : STRING;
                      DOB   : birthday;
                  END;
```

123

```
VAR
    list : ARRAY [1..5] OF Names_Dates;
    index : INTEGER;
BEGIN
    WriteLn('Input name and date of birth for five people');
    FOR index: = 1 TO 5 DO
    BEGIN
        Write('NAME ');
        ReadLn(list[index].name);
        Write('DATE OF BIRTH ');
        ReadLn(list[index].DOB.day, list[index].DOB.month, list[index].DOB.year);
    END; {FOR}
    {output the contents of the array}
    FOR index: = 1 TO 5 DO
        WriteLn( list[index].name,
                 list[index].DOB.day:3,
                 list[index].DOB.month:3,
                 list[index].DOB.year:5);
    {END FOR}
END. {RecordDemo}
```

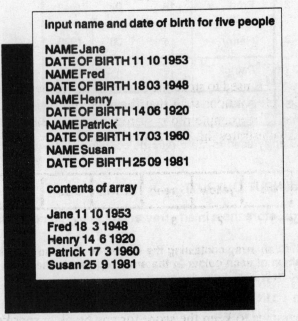

The amount of coding required to access a field within a record can be quite cumbersome. Consider the duplication of code necessary in displaying the fields for day, month and year in this program. A shorthand way of reducing the redundant code is to use a WITH statement. The code:

```
FOR index:=1 TO 5 DO
    WriteLn( list[index].name,
             list[index].DOB.day:3,
             list[index].DOB.month:3,
             list[index].DOB.year:5);
{END FOR}
```

can be reduced to:

```
FOR index:=1 TO 5 DO
    WITH list[index] DO
        WriteLn(name, DOB.day:3, DOB.month:3, DOB.year:5);
{END FOR}
```

or even:

```
FOR index:=1 TO 5 DO
    WITH list[index] DO
    BEGIN
        Write(name);
        WITH DOB DO
            WriteLn(day:3, month:3, year:5);
    END; {WITH}
{END FOR}
```

7.6 Worked examples

In the first example an array is used to store the names of the coloured balls in a game of snooker. The names are stored in cell positions such that the subscript or index to the cell represents the value of the coloured ball. For example red is stored in cell 1, yellow in cell 2, green in cell 3, .. black in cell 7. Figure 7.10 illustrates this data stored in the array.

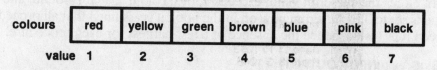

colours	red	yellow	green	brown	blue	pink	black
value	1	2	3	4	5	6	7

figure 7.10 an array containing the names of coloured balls in snooker
the position of each colour in the array represents the value of that
coloured ball

The purpose of the program is to keep the score for any break in snooker. The user is invited to type the colour of the ball potted, its corresponding value is displayed, followed by the total for the break. For each ball potted the total for the break is increased by the value of the ball until the user inputs the word NONE to signify the end of the break.

The procedure search is used to compare the colour of the ball potted with each colour stored in the array. If a match between colours is found then the value for that ball can be determined, otherwise no value is assumed for the colour potted.

Notice that in the procedure to search for a colour it was not prudent to use a for..do loop to access each cell of the array until a match for the colour had been found. Had a for..do loop been used then an alternative way of coding the loop within the search procedure might have been as follows.

```
FOR value:=1 TO 7 DO
   IF pot = colours[value] THEN
   BEGIN
      score:=value;
      found:=TRUE;
   END; {IF}
END; {FOR}
```

If the value for pot had been 'black', then this coding is perfectly satisfactory since the colour match is not found until value is 7, that is at the extreme end of the array. But what if the colour had been 'red'? The score would be set to 1 and found to true, then it would be necessary to go round the loop a further six times testing if there was a colour match. Clearly this would be a waste of time!

An improvement to the coding can be achieved in several ways, however, the most satisfactory method in Pascal is to replace the for..do loop with a while..do loop, and include a test in the while loop as to whether the colour has not been found. In addition to this test it is necessary to include a test for the index or subscript to the array going out of bounds (value <=7). Combining the two conditions creates the statement:

WHILE (value <= 7) AND NOT found DO

Initially if found is set to FALSE and value is set to 1, the contents of the loop will continue to be executed until either the subscript value exceeds 7, or a colour match is found, and the Boolean variable found is set to TRUE. From now on in the book it is assumed that all procedures that are listed have been fully tested, hence the absence of a test harness for each procedure.

```
PROGRAM BigBreak(INPUT, OUTPUT);
{
program to calculate the amount scored in a break in snooker
}
TYPE
   ArrayOfColour = ARRAY[1..7] OF STRING;

VAR
   colours      : ArrayOfColour;
   pot          : STRING;
   break, score : INTEGER;
   found        : BOOLEAN;
```

126

```
PROCEDURE initialise(VAR colours:ArrayOfColour);
{
procedure to store each colour in consecutive cells of the array such that the array subscript
represents the value of the ball
}
BEGIN
    colours[1]:='red';
    colours[2]:='yellow';
    colours[3]:='green';
    colours[4]:='brown';
    colours[5]:='blue';
    colours[6]:='pink';
    colours[7]:='black';
END; {initialise}

PROCEDURE PotBall(VAR pot : STRING);
{
procedure to input the colour of the potted ball
}
BEGIN
    Write('input potted colour - type NONE to end break ');
    ReadLn(pot);
END; {PotBall}

PROCEDURE results(score : INTEGER; break : INTEGER);
{
procedure to display the value of the ball potted and the current value of the break
}
BEGIN
    WriteLn(pot, ' potted score ', score:2);
    WriteLn('break score ', break:3);
END; {results}

PROCEDURE search(pot : STRING;VAR score:INTEGER;VAR colours: ArrayOfColour;
                 VAR found : BOOLEAN);
{
procedure to search an array for the name of a colour, when found the position of the colour is
the score for that ball
}
VAR
    value : INTEGER;
BEGIN
    found:=FALSE;
    value:=1;
    WHILE (value <=7) AND NOT found DO
        IF pot = colours[value] THEN
        BEGIN
            score:=value;
            found:=TRUE;
        END
```

```
        ELSE
            value:=value+1;
        {END IF}
      {END WHILE}
END; {search}

BEGIN
    initialise(colours);
    break:=0;
    PotBall(pot);
    WHILE pot < > 'NONE' DO
    BEGIN
        search(pot, score, colours, found);
        IF found THEN
        BEGIN
            break:=break+score;
            results(score, break);
        END; {IF}
        PotBall(pot);
    END; {WHILE}
END. {BigBreak}
```

```
input potted colour - type NONE to end break red
red potted score 1
break score 1
input potted colour - type NONE to end break black
black potted score 7
break score 8
input potted colour - type NONE to end break red
red potted score 1
break score 9
input potted colour - type NONE to end break blue
blue potted score 5
break score 14
input potted colour - type NONE to end break NONE
```

The second program in this section is an improvement of the palindrome example given in section 7.4. Not only has the program been developed as a set of procedures, which of course is only good practice, but each character of the word that is input is changed to an upper case character. If this conversion had not been made then a letter in lower case when compared with the same letter in upper case would in the case of a palindrome give the wrong result. For example with this modification the word raDAr would be detected as a palindrome.

Notice that in the procedure to test a word for being a palindrome that a for..do loop has not been used on purpose, so as to avoid the problem of continued repetition when there is not a character match.

```
PROGRAM palindrome(INPUT, OUTPUT);
{
Improved program to input a word and test whether it is a palindrome
}
VAR
    word                : STRING;
    CharactersMatch  : BOOLEAN;

PROCEDURE InputWord(VAR word : STRING);
{
Input a word and change every letter to upper case
}
VAR
    index           : INTEGER;
    ASCIIcode    : INTEGER;
BEGIN
    Write('Input one word ');
    ReadLn(word);
    FOR index: = 1 TO ORD(word[0]) DO
    BEGIN
        ASCIIcode: = ORD(word[index]);
        {test for lower case letter in range a .. z}
        IF (ASCIIcode > = 97) AND (ASCIIcode < = 122) THEN
        BEGIN
            ASCIIcode:=ASCIIcode-32;
            word[index]:=CHR(ASCIIcode);
        END; {IF}
    END; {FOR}
END; {InputWord}


PROCEDURE test(word : STRING; VAR CharactersMatch : BOOLEAN);
{
test for palindrome
}
VAR
    index1, index2 : INTEGER;

BEGIN
    index1:=1;
    index2:=ORD(word[0]);
    CharactersMatch:=TRUE;
    WHILE (index1 < = index2) AND CharactersMatch DO
        IF word[index1] = word[index2] THEN
        BEGIN
            index1:=index1+1;
            index2:=index2-1;
        END
        ELSE
            CharactersMatch:=FALSE;
        {END IF}
    {END WHILE}
END; {test}
```

```
PROCEDURE result(word : STRING; CharactersMatch : BOOLEAN);
{
output result of test
}
BEGIN
   IF CharactersMatch THEN
       WriteLn(word, ' is a palindrome')
   ELSE
       WriteLn(word, ' is NOT a palindrome');
   {END IF}
END; {result}

{main program}
BEGIN
   InputWord(word);
   test(word, CharactersMatch);
   result(word, CharactersMatch);
END. {palindrome}
```

```
input one word  raDAr
RADAR is a palindrome
Input one word  MouSE
MOUSE is NOT a palindrome
```

The final program in this section is an extension of the program to create an array of names and dates of birth. Having input the data and stored it in an array, the user is invited to type the name of a person, the array is searched for that name, and if a match is found the date of birth for that person is displayed.

Once again in the procedure to search for a name a for..do loop has not been used, so to prevent an unnecessary number of repetitions of the loop after a person's name has been matched with a name in the array.

```
PROGRAM RecordDemo(INPUT, OUTPUT);
{
program to create records, store them in an array and search the array for a name and display
the date of birth
}
TYPE
   birthday =  RECORD
                day     : INTEGER;
                month   : INTEGER;
                year    : INTEGER;
              END;
```

```
    Names_Dates =    RECORD
                        name : STRING;
                        DOB : birthday;
                     END;
    Many_Names_Dates = ARRAY [1..5] OF Names_Dates;
VAR
    list : Many_Names_Dates;
    person : STRING;
    found : BOOLEAN;
    position_in_array : INTEGER;
    NoMoreData : BOOLEAN;

PROCEDURE InputData(VAR list : Many_Names_Dates);
{
create an array of names and corresponding birthdays
}
VAR
    index : INTEGER;

BEGIN
    WriteLn('Input name and date of birth for five people');
    FOR index:=1 TO 5 DO
    BEGIN
        Write('NAME ');
        ReadLn(list[index].name);
        Write('DATE OF BIRTH ');
        ReadLn(list[index].DOB.day, list[index].DOB.month, list[index].DOB.year);
    END; {FOR}
END; {InputData}


PROCEDURE InputName(VAR person:STRING);
{
input the name of a person whose birthday is to be looked up
}
BEGIN
    Write('Input name of person ');
    ReadLn(person);
END; {InputName}


PROCEDURE search(list : Many_Names_Dates; person: STRING;
                 VAR found: BOOLEAN; VAR position_in_array : INTEGER);
{
search for a matching name of person and if found return the position in the array of the match
}
BEGIN
    position_in_array := 1;
    found := FALSE;
    WHILE (position_in_array <= 5) AND NOT found DO
    IF person = list[position_in_array].name THEN
```

131

```
                found:=TRUE
        ELSE
            position_in_array := position_in_array + 1;
        {END IF}
    {END WHILE}
END; {search}

PROCEDURE continue(VAR NoMoreData : BOOLEAN);
{
ask whether user wishes to continue
}
VAR
reply : STRING;

BEGIN
    Write('do you want to continue? - answer yes or no ');
    ReadLn(reply);
    IF (reply = 'no') OR (reply = 'NO') OR (reply = 'n') OR (reply = 'N') THEN
        NoMoreData := TRUE
    ELSE
        NoMoreData := FALSE;
    {END IF}
END; {continue}

BEGIN
    InputData(list);
    REPEAT
        InputName(person);
        search(list, person, found, position_in_array);
        IF found THEN
            WriteLn('date of birth ',   list[position_in_array].DOB.day:3,
                                        list[position_in_array].DOB.month:3,
                                        list[position_in_array].DOB.year:5)

        ELSE
            WriteLn(person, ' not in list');
        {END IF}
        continue(NoMoreData);
    UNTIL NoMoreData;
END. {RecordDemo}
```

132

```
Input name and date of birth for five people

NAME Jane
DATE OF BIRTH 11 10 1953
NAME Fred
DATE OF BIRTH 18 03 1948
NAME Henry
DATE OF BIRTH 14 06 1920
NAME Patrick
DATE OF BIRTH 17 03 1960
NAME Susan
DATE OF BIRTH 25 09 1981

Input name of person Henry
date of birth 14  6 1920
do you want to continue? - answer yes or no yes
Input name of person George
George not in list
do you want to continue? - answer yes or no yes
Input name of person Patrick
date of birth 17  3 1960
do you want to continue? - answer yes or no yes
Input name of person Jane
date of birth 11 10 1953
do you want to continue? - answer yes or no no
```

7.7 Summary

● A for..do loop provides a straightforward way of using a loop control variable as a counter.

● A for..do loop automatically initialises the loop control variable to the lower limit, tests the variable to see if it has reached the upper limit, and increases the value of the control variable by one. When the value of the loop control variable exceeds the value of the upper limit the computer exits from the loop to the next executable statement after the end of the body of the loop.

● The value of the loop control variable is either increased by one if the lower limit is less than the upper limit, or decreased by 1 if the lower limit is greater than the upper limit. In the latter case the reserved word TO must be replaced by DOWNTO.

● A one-dimensional array is a data structure that can be used to store data of the same type.

● An array is subdivided into cells, with each cell having a unique subscript or index value.

● The maximum number of cells that an array contains is declared in a program and remains constant. For this reason an array is known as a static data structure.

● Access to any item of data in the array is through the name of the array, followed by the position of the data in the array, that is the subscript or index value of the cell that contains the data.

● A loop control variable in a for..do statement is a useful way of representing the subscript or index of an array. By varying the value of the loop control variable it is possible to access any cell within the array.

● Never use a for..do loop when searching for an item of data in an array, since the loop will not terminate when the item is found, unless the item happens to be the last item in the array.

● A variable of string data type is represented as an array of characters. However, the size of the array changes according to the length of the string. For this reason an array used to store a string is known as a dynamic array, and is not the same data type as a predefined array of characters. However, in Turbo Pascal this restriction is lifted, and both data types are compatible.

● The contents of a variable of string data type can be accessed as individual characters stored from cell 1 in a one-dimensional array.

● In Turbo Pascal the length of a string is automatically stored as a character representation in cell 0.

● A record is a data type.

● A collection of data, of possibly different types, can be stored in a variable having a predefined record structure.

● The individual parts of a record are known as data fields. To access a specific field the variable name associated with the record must be qualified with the name of the field.

● To simplify the qualification of a variable name with a field name a WITH statement may be used.

● By creating an array of records it is possible to store data of different types in an array.

7.8 Questions

1. Write programs using for..do loops to:

     a. Display the numbers 50 to 75 with an incremental value of 1.

     b. Display the numbers 20 to 5 with an incremental value of -1.

c. Display the odd integers in the range 1 to 29 inclusive.

d. Display the squares of the even integers in the range 2 to 20 inclusive.

e. Display the sum of the squares of the odd integers in the range 1 to 13 inclusive.

f. Display the lower case letters of the alphabet a, through z, and the upper case letters of the alphabet, in reverse Z through A.

2. Write a program to store the alphabet as characters in an array. The program should display:

a. The entire alphabet.

b. The first six characters of the alphabet.

c. The last ten characters of the alphabet.

d. The tenth character of the alphabet.

3. A one-dimensional array X contains eight integers already sorted into ascending order. Write a program to copy the numbers from array X to another one-dimensional array Y such that array Y contains the numbers in descending order.

4. Write a program to input and store in an array, ten records that contain the names of telephone exchanges and their corresponding STD codes. For example Oxford 0865 might be one record in the array. Include a procedure to search for the name of the exchange when given the STD code. Display the result of the search.

5. Write a procedure to store only the score-draws of football matches in a one- dimensional array. The maximum number of matches played is fifty-eight, and the results are recorded as the Boolean value TRUE for a score-draw, otherwise the Boolean value FALSE.

If one line on the football pools is stored in another one-dimensional array as twelve predicted score-draws by integers in the range 1 to 58, corresponding to the matches being played, check the contents of this array for the number of score draws that actually happened, and display this result.

6. Write a program to store the names of foods and their prices, as displayed in the Greasy Spoon Cafe (section 1.1), as records in an array. Extend the program to:

a. Input the name of an item of food and display the price.

b. Input an amount of money and display all the individual items of food that cost the same or less than the amount of money.

c. Generate a fully itemised bill, similar to that shown in section 2.8.

7. From the saying "thirty days hath September, April, June and November, and all the rest have thirty-one , except for February that has twenty-eight days clear and twenty-nine in a Leap Year", write a program to:

a. store the names and number of days in each month as records in an array;

b. display a calendar for any year remaining in the twentieth century (1993 .. 1999), printing the year and the names of the months; the value for the date is to be printed under the name of the day.

8.
Files of information

This chapter explores an alternative method of storing data using files. Two different file formats are examined, together with a method of sorting the data in files and writing reports.

Contents

8.1 Text files

A text data file is stored in the same character format as a source program file.

A text file is a stream of ASCII characters, divided into lines, each with an end of line marker, which is a carriage-return character, possibly followed by a line-feed character.

There are two ways in which a text file may be created. The first is by using the system editor in the same way as a program is created, via keyboard entry, with the text file stored on magnetic disc. The second is from within a program by using Write and WriteLn statements to direct output to, normally a text file held on magnetic disc, instead of the screen.

A program heading defines two system text files called INPUT and OUTPUT. A stream of characters input at a keyboard and output to a screen can be thought of as the contents of the text files INPUT and OUTPUT respectively. Text files, however, are not confined to keyboard input and screen output, they can be read from or written to secondary storage media, such as magnetic discs.

The method of redirecting the input and output is through the program heading. The INPUT and OUTPUT system file declarations are replaced by the explicit names of the text files being used. For example, PROGRAM insured(data, results); specifies two files, *data* and *results*, that are used in place of INPUT and OUTPUT. The two files must be declared as variables of type TEXT.

```
VAR
   data      : TEXT;
   results   : TEXT;
```

The inclusion of text files does not prohibit the use of the system files INPUT and OUTPUT. For a program that reads data from both the keyboard and a file called *data*, and writes information to both the screen and a file called *results*, the program heading would be modified to:

PROGRAM identifier(INPUT, data, OUTPUT, results);

However, only the *data* and *results* files are declared as variables of type TEXT.

8.2 File processing activities

Opening a file

Before a file can be used it must be opened for either reading or writing by using the predefined procedures RESET and REWRITE respectively. RESET(data) opens a file called *data* ready for reading from the first line; REWRITE(report) opens a file called *report* for writing, or overwriting existing lines, which in effect initialises the file to contain zero lines of text.

Figure 8.1 illustrates that after the file named *data* has been opened, the *file position* is set to the first line in the file.

Warning! Either RESET or REWRITE must not be used with the system files INPUT and OUTPUT, since these files are automatically opened for keyboard input and screen output.

In Turbo Pascal it is necessary to assign the filename used in the program to the filename in the directory. For example, the statement ASSIGN(data, 'B:DATA.TXT'); will assign the text file *data* to the ASCII character file named DATA.TXT stored on drive B of a personal computer.

Warning! In Turbo Pascal, all disc-based text files must be assigned to a file held in the directory of a disc drive before either RESET or REWRITE can be used.

	text file - data	EOF(data)	ReadLn(data, price, appliance)
file position →	395.95 television 550.00 music centre 149.95 freezer	FALSE	price = 395.95 appliance = television
file position →	395.95 television 550.00 music centre 149.95 freezer	FALSE	price = 550.00 appliance = music centre
file position →	395.95 television 550.00 music centre 149.95 freezer	FALSE	price = 149.95 appliance = freezer
file position →	395.95 television 550.00 music centre 149.95 freezer	TRUE	

Figure 8.1 reading lines in a text file

Reading a text file

The lines of a text file can be read by using Read and ReadLn. However, the statements are modified by including the name of the file to be read. For example, the statement **ReadLn(data,price,appliance);** would read a real value for price and a string value for appliance from a line of the text file, that might contain the data depicted in figure 8.1.

Detecting the end of a file

The repeated execution of Read/ ReadLn statements will cause all the data in the file to be read and an attempt would be made to read beyond the end of the file. This will result in a run-time error and the program will be terminated by the operating system. Therefore, it is important that a method should exist for detecting the end of the file. The Boolean function end of file EOF, is TRUE when the file position is beyond the last line(ie at the end of the file), otherwise, it returns a value of FALSE. Since the file position is initially positioned at the first line to be read, any attempt to open an empty file would result in the file position pointing at the end of the file, and the value of the function EOF would be TRUE.

Notice from figure 8.1 that the function EOF is TRUE after the last line in the file has been read.

Writing to a file

Information is written to a file by the use of Write and WriteLn. However, the statements are modified by including the name of the file. For example, the statement WriteLn(results, price:7:2, appliance); would append the information for the price and the name of the appliance to the file called results. Continued use of this statement would result in many lines containing prices and names of appliances to be written to the file.

Closing a file

There is no predefined procedure in Standard Pascal to close a file. The mode of use of a file is changed by opening the file again, even though it is in effect still open. A file opened for writing by REWRITE is changed to reading by RESET. When lines are written to a file, the last few lines although created, do not always get transferred from the system output buffer to the file. In order to flush the lines from the buffer and append them to the file being created, a RESET statement should be used, in effect, to close the file.

8.3 Reading and writing

A text file contains the following lines of data that relate to the insured values of several domestic appliances. For example, a television is insured for £395.95, a music centre is insured for £550.00, etc.

```
395.95 television
550.00 music centre
995.95 desk-top computer
199.95 microwave oven
299.99 washing machine
149.95 freezer
```

The first program demonstrates how to open the file, and read and display the contents line by line.

```
PROGRAM TextFile(data, OUTPUT);
{
program to read the contents of a text file called data and display the contents of the file on the
screen
}
```

```
VAR
    price       : REAL;
    appliance   : STRING;
    data        : TEXT;
BEGIN
    {open the data file}
    ASSIGN(data, 'B:DATA.TXT');
    RESET(data);

    WHILE NOT EOF(data) DO
    BEGIN
        ReadLn(data, price, appliance);
        WriteLn(price:7:2, appliance);
    END; {WHILE}

    {close data file}
    RESET(data);
END.{TextFile}
```

```
395.95    television
550.00    music centre
995.95    desk-top computer
199.95    microwave oven
299.99    washing machine
149.95    freezer
```

When using files output does not necessarily need to be directed to a screen, it can in fact be directed to another text file. In the next example the contents of the file used in the previous program is modified such that the value of each appliance is increased by the rate of inflation, and the new value together with the name of the appliance is written to a text file.

```
PROGRAM TextFiles(OldData, NewData);
{
program to read the price and name of a domestic appliance from a text file called OldData,
increase the price of the appliance by the rate of inflation and write the new price and appliance
name to a new text file called NewData
}
CONST
    inflation = 0.025; {rate of inflation 2.5%}
VAR
    price       : REAL;
    appliance   : STRING;
    OldData     : TEXT;
    NewData     : TEXT;
BEGIN
    {open the data file}
    ASSIGN(OldData, 'b:data.txt');
```

```
    RESET(OldData);
    {open the inflated data file}
    ASSIGN(NewData, 'b:NewData.txt');
    REWRITE(NewData);

    WHILE NOT EOF(OldData) DO
    BEGIN
        ReadLn(OldData, price, appliance);
        price:=price+(price*inflation);
        WriteLn(NewData, price:7:2, appliance);
    END; {WHILE}

    {close data files}
    RESET(OldData);
    RESET(NewData);
END.{TextFiles}
```

The output shows the contents of the file NewData.

```
405.85    television
563.75    music centre
1020.85   desk-top computer
204.95    microwave oven
307.49    washing machine
153.70    freezer
```

8.4 Sort utility

The reader should be well aware of the need to present information in a usable form. Consider the organisation of a telephone directory, entries are ordered into strict alphabetical sequence by name. To find a telephone number, knowing the name of the person you want to call, is simply a matter of locating the appropriate section of the directory from the first few letters of the surname, and then searching several pages until a match is found for the surname. The address and telephone number of the person will be listed against the surname.

Another example of the organisation of information is that of a bus timetable. A timetable is organised into bus routes, often in ascending order of bus number, for example 131, 137, 137A, etc. For each bus route a chronological listing of bus departure times from a bus station, with arrival and departure times at places on route are given. Each route will normally have separate entries for buses travelling in opposite directions. If the time of a bus is to be found the bus number can easily be referenced since these are displayed in an ordered sequence. Departure times are listed chronologically, making reference to a specific part of the day simple. Bus arrival and departure times can then be selected from that part of the timetable.

In both these examples the information is required to be ordered or sorted on a part of the information. Telephone directories are sorted on names, bus timetables are sorted on bus routes and times of day. Such information is said to have been sorted on a key. Names of people, bus routes and times of the day all being examples of keys to information.

Computers are capable of storing very large amounts of information, and it is very important that the information is kept in an ordered format to provide fast access to information given an appropriate key and to allow for an orderly presentation of information when producing reports.

MSDOS provides a means of sorting the contents of text files into order. For example the file B:DATA.TXT created in the previous example, can be sorted into sequence by price, and stored in a different file named B:PRICE.TXT, by using the SORT command. For example:

C:> **SORT <B:DATA.TXT >B:PRICE.TXT** and the contents of B:PRICE.TXT would then appear as:

```
149.95 freezer
199.95 microwave oven
299.99 washing machine
395.95 television
550.00 music centre
995.95 desk-top computer
```

Since the price of an appliance starts in column 1, each line of the text file has been ordered by digits (the price). However, if it was required to sort the file into order by name of appliance then it is possible to state at which column sorting should take place. For example:

C:> **SORT /+8 <B:DATA.TXT >B:NAME.TXT** and the contents of B:NAME.TXT would then appear as:

```
995.95 desk-top computer
149.95 freezer
199.95 microwave oven
550.00 music centre
395.95 television
299.99 washing machine
```

The order of this file could also be reversed by modifying the command to:

C:> **SORT /r/+8 <B:DATA.TXT >B:NAME.TXT** and the contents of B:NAME.TXT would then appear as:

```
299.99 washing machine
395.95 television
550.00 music centre
199.95 microwave oven
149.95 freezer
995.95 desk-top computer
```

The reader is advised to refer to their MSDOS manual for further information about the SORT utility.

8.5 Report writing

Directing output to a screen is fine for a small amount of data, however, since the output scrolls off the screen, it is of little use if the file contains a considerable number of lines. Printed output on paper, of the contents of the file, is usually more acceptable. With Pascal it is possible to direct the output that normally appears on a screen to a text file stored on magnetic disc. The contents of the text file can, at the users request, be printed on the paper.

For example if a text file had been created using the name B:REPORT.TXT then to obtain a print-out of the report in a PC-based environment, the following commands should be given from MSDOS, C:> **PRINT B:REPORT.TXT.** Provided a printer is connected on-line, the contents of the report will be output to the printer. If you have difficulties printing a text file then refer to your MSDOS manual for more information.

The following text file has been created using an editor, sorted into alphabetical sequence and stored under the name B:BOOKS.TXT. Each line in the file contains the title of a book, the quantity in stock and the price of the book. Notice from the listing of this file that the contents of the three fields, title, quantity and price each take up a fixed amount of space. It is possible to define the field width of a STRING by specifying the maximum number of characters in the field after the type declaration of the string variable for that field. For example, VAR title : STRING[20]; where 20 indicates that the size of the field for title will always be 20 characters, and this includes the spaces. When declaring numbers in a text file the field width is not important since each number is separated from the next by at least one space.

```
Art in Athens        1 8.95
Birds of Prey        2 3.75
Eagles of Scotland   1 7.50
Gone with the Wind   3 5.20
Hate, Lust and Love  2 3.75
Maths for Adults     3 5.95
Modern Farming       3 3.75
Raiders of Planet X  3 5.20
Splitting the Atom   1 8.95
The Invisible Man    1 3.75
The Otter            2 3.75
The Tempest          4 5.95
The Trojan Wars      2 5.95
Under the Seas       2 3.75
Vampire Bats         2 7.50
```

A report is to be printed on the contents of this file. The design of a report is made considerably easier if the reader adopts the habit of planning the layout of the report on a report layout sheet, similar to the one shown in figure 8.2. If such a document cannot be obtained then paper pre-ruled into squares with numbered columns can be used. Such a document is an aid towards coding the Write and WriteLn statements in a program. Notice from the design of the document that when the stock level falls to one item the report indicates that the stock should be replenished. Notice also that totals are calculated for the number of books and value of all the books in stock and printed at the end of the report.

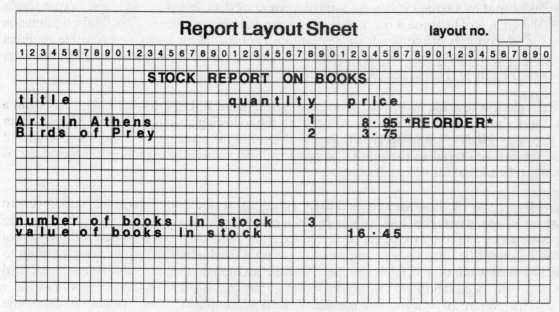

Figure 8.2 layout of a report file

```
PROGRAM StockReport(books, report);
{
program to read a file containing a stock list of books and print the contents of the file, showing
which books to reorder, and the total number of books together with the total value of the stock
}
CONST
    ReorderLevel = 1;
VAR
    title           : STRING[20];
    quantity        : INTEGER;
    price           : REAL;
    books           : TEXT;
    report          : TEXT;
    TotalQuantity   : INTEGER;
    TotalPrice      : REAL;
BEGIN
    {open book and report files}
    ASSIGN(books, 'B:BOOKS.TXT');
    RESET(books);
    ASSIGN(report, 'B:REPORT.TXT');
    REWRITE(report);
```

145

```
TotalQuantity: = 0;TotalPrice: =0;

{report headings}
WriteLn(report, ' STOCK REPORT ON BOOKS'); WriteLn(report);
WriteLn(report, 'title quantity price'); WriteLn(report);

{process book file}
WHILE NOT EOF(books) DO
BEGIN
    ReadLn(books, title, quantity, price);
    Write(report, title, quantity:8, price:8:2);
    IF quantity < = ReorderLevel THEN
        WriteLn(report, ' * REORDER * ')
    ELSE
        WriteLn(report);
    {END IF}
    TotalQuantity: =TotalQuantity + quantity;
    TotalPrice: =TotalPrice + (price * quantity);
END; {WHILE}

WriteLn(report);
WriteLn(report, 'number of books in stock ', TotalQuantity:3);
WriteLn(report, 'value of books in stock £', TotalPrice:6:2);
{close file}
RESET(report);
END. {StockReport}
```

```
                STOCK REPORT ON BOOKS

        title                   quantity    price

        Art in Athens               1       8.95    *REORDER*
        Birds of Prey               2       3.75
        Eagles of Scotland          1       7.50    *REORDER*
        Gone with the Wind          3       5.20
        Hate, Lust and Love         2       3.75
        Maths for Adults            3       5.95
        Modern Farming              3       3.75
        Raiders of Planet X         3       5.20
        Splitting the Atom          1       8.95    *REORDER*
        The Invisible Man           1       3.75    *REORDER*
        The Otter                   2       3.75
        The Tempest                 4       5.95
        The Trojan Wars             2       5.95
        Under the Seas              2       3.75
        Vampire Bats                2       7.50

        number of books in stock   32
        value of books in stock           £170.15
```

8.6 Direct access file

In the previous example if it had been required to search the books file for a particular title, it would have been necessary to compare the title in each line of the file until the required title was found or the end of the file was reached. There was no relationship between a book title and its position in the file.

With a direct access file the key to each record is translated by the computer into the position in the file where the record is stored. Therefore knowing the key to a record means that access to that record is direct without having to search through the keys of the other records in the file.

The format of a direct access file is different to a text file in that it uses records and not lines of text.

A direct access file must be declared as a FILE OF records of a particular type. For example:

```
TYPE
    information =   RECORD
                    artist    : STRING[18];
                    title     : STRING[33];
                    duration : REAL;
                    END;

    CD = FILE OF information;
```

It is then possible to declare the name of the direct access file as a variable of the same type:

```
VAR
    disc        : CD;
```

The file processing statements used for text files can also be used for direct access files, therefore, the statements ASSIGN, RESET, REWRITE and EOF are used in the same context as for text files. Records in a direct access file are read using a *Read* statement and written using a *Write* statement.

The only new activity associated with direct access files in Pascal is to change the current file position to the position of the record to be processed, having first specified the key to the record. A direct access record key is a positive integer that represents the relative position of a record with respect to the beginning of the file. For example, a record with a key value of 10 represents the record occupying the tenth record area in the file, irrespective of whether the record areas 1 through 9 have been filled.

The Pascal statement used to change the current file position is **SEEK(filename, record key);** and is used prior to reading from or writing to the file.

Direct access to files is non-standard in Pascal, therefore different compilers support different implementations of this method.

Turbo Pascal numbers its direct access records from 0 and not from 1.

Turbo Pascal has two predefined functions FILEPOS which returns the current position of the file, and FILESIZE which returns the current size of the file.

Warning! The format of a direct access file is different to a text file in that it uses records and not lines of text.

In the following example data from both a text file and a direct access file are processed. A compact disc player enables the user to select the tracks of a compact disc in random order. This idea can be incorporated into a program to demonstrate the use of a direct access file in allowing a user to select any track at random and the artist's name, title of the song/tune and length of playing time to be displayed on a screen.

A text file contains the following information taken from the compact disc 'Soulemotion' from Polygram Record Operations Ltd. Each line corresponds to one line in the text file, and is ordered by track number starting at track 1, followed by track 2, etc.

Simply Red	If you don't know me by now	3.23
Robert Palmer	Mercy, mercy me/ I want you	4.48
Paul Young	Wherever I lay my hat	4.09
Tina Turner	Let's stay together	3.35
Lisa Stansfield	Change	4.14
Whitney Houston	One moment in time	4.43
Dionne Warwick	Walk on by	2.46
Stephanie Mills	Never knew love like this before	3.22
Omar	There's nothing like this	3.57
Kenny Thomas	Thinking about your love	4.51
Cathy Dennis	Too many walls	4.22
Quartz	It's too late	4.00
Phyllis Nelson	Move closer	4.13
James Brown	It's a man's man's man's world	2.46
Wilson Pickett	In the midnight hour	2.26
Barry White	Can't get enough of your love	4.01
Earth Wind & Fire	After the love has gone	4.33
Ashford&Simpson	Solid	3.23

This information is transferred one line at a time to the fields of a record, and the record is copied to a direct access file at a position specified by the track number.

```
ReadLn(data, CD_entry.artist, CD_entry.title, CD_entry.duration);
SEEK(disc, track);
Write(disc, CD_entry);
```

When all the records have been copied to the direct access file it is possible to access this file directly by specifying the track number.

```
SEEK(disc, track);
Read(disc, CD_entry);
```

```
PROGRAM DirectAccess(INPUT, OUTPUT, data, disc);
{
program to read a file containing the name of an artist, song and the length of the song, and
transfer this information to a direct access file. The contents of the file can then be inspected,
track by track
}
TYPE
    information =  RECORD
                        artist   : STRING[18];
                        title    : STRING[33];
                        duration : REAL;
                    END;
    CD = FILE OF information;
VAR
    data        : TEXT;
    disc        : CD;
    CD_entry    : information;
    track       : INTEGER;
BEGIN
    {transfer contents of text file to direct access file}
    ASSIGN(data,'B:MUSIC.TXT');
    RESET(data);
    ASSIGN(disc,'B:DISC.DAF');
    REWRITE(disc);
    track:=1;
    WHILE NOT EOF(data) DO
    BEGIN
        ReadLn(data, CD_entry.artist, CD_entry.title, CD_entry.duration);
        SEEK(disc, track);
        Write(disc, CD_entry);
        track:=track+1;
    END; {WHILE}
    RESET(disc);
    REPEAT
        Write('track? '); ReadLn(track);
        IF (track > 0) AND (track <= FILESIZE(disc)-1) THEN
        BEGIN
            SEEK(disc, track);
            IF NOT EOF(disc) THEN Read(disc, CD_entry);
            WITH CD_entry DO
            BEGIN
                WriteLn('artist: ', artist);
                WriteLn('title: ', title);
                WriteLn('duration: ', duration:5:2);
            END;
            WriteLn;
        END; {IF}
    UNTIL track <= 0;
END. {DirectAccess}
```

```
track? 3
artist: Paul Young
title: Wherever I lay my hat
duration: 4.09

track? 10
artist: Kenny Thomas
title: Thinking about your love
duration: 4.51

track? 5
artist: Lisa Stansfield
title: Change
duration: 4.14

track? 0
```

8.7 Summary

● A stream of ASCII characters, read line by line, from an input device, such as a magnetic disc, is a text file.

● Similarly a stream of ASCII characters, written line by line, to an output device, such as a printer or magnetic disc, is a text file.

● The reserved words INPUT and OUTPUT are used to represent the keyboard and screen system text files respectively.

● With the exception of INPUT and OUTPUT, all text files must be opened before use. In Turbo Pascal it is necessary to ASSIGN the MSDOS name of the file to the Pascal name before it can be opened.

● Whenever a file is opened, the file position is set to the first line to be read, or at the beginning of the file to be written.

● Whenever a ReadLn statement that refers to a file is executed, the file position is automatically advanced to the next line, until it points to the end of the file.

● An end of file function will return the value TRUE when the file position points beyond the last line of the file.

● Text is written to a file one item after another in the order in which the Write and WriteLn statements occur in a program.

● Whenever a file is no longer required it should be closed. There is no predefined procedure in Standard Pascal to close a file. Files opened for writing should be closed with RESET to ensure that the last line of the file is written. RESET changes the mode of the file from writing to reading, and the file position is re-positioned at the beginning of the file.

● Before programming the output for a report, the layout of the report should first be designed on squared paper. The layout of the information can then be transferred directly into the appropriate Write and WriteLn statements.

● Whenever possible data should be stored sorted.

● A direct access file is a file of records and NOT a text file.

● A direct access record key, which must be a positive integer, is used to access the appropriate record in such a file organisation.

● The record in the file is accessed directly by using a SEEK statement that contains the value of the numeric key.

● Turbo Pascal contains two predefined functions FILEPOS to return the current position of the file, and FILESIZE which returns the current size of the file.

8.8 Questions

1. Use an editor to create a text file containing words and their meanings, with a word and its meaning written on one line. The size of a word should be less than fifteen characters and the size of the meaning less than 50 characters.

Use the MSDOS SORT utility, or equivalent, to order the file into alphabetical sequence using the word as the key.

After the file has been created, write a program to read and display the contents of the file;

2. Create a file containing the details of telephone subscribers. Lines are of fixed length and contain the following details.

surname and initials	: 20 characters
telephone number	: 20 characters
previous meter reading	: integer
current meter reading	: integer

Invent a minimum of ten test data lines containing the data described. Assume that the previous meter reading is always less than the current meter reading. Using an editor, input and store the lines into a text file. Using a sorting utility, such as SORT in MSDOS, order the file on surname and initials as primary key.

Using the ordered text file write a program to output the following report. Assume that charges for telephone calls are £0.04 per unit.

TELEPHONE SUBSCRIBERS

NAME	NUMBER	UNITS USED	CHARGE £
Allen P	Abingdon 41937	2719	108.76
Brown J	Oxford 2245643	645	25.80
Carter F	Banbury 212	1768	70.72
.	.	.	.
.	.	.	.

3. Create a file that contains the details of items of stock in a brewery. Lines are of fixed length and contain the following details.

stock number	: 5 characters
description	: 25 characters
stock quantity	: integer
unit price	: real

Assume that the lines are not in stock number order when they are input into the computer. Limit the number of test data lines to ten in this question. Using an editor, input and store the test data in a text file. Using an external sorting package, such as SORT in MSDOS, order the contents of the file on the stock number as primary key.

Using the ordered text file write a program to output the following report.

STOCK REPORT

STOCK NUMBER	DESCRIPTION	UNIT COST	LEVEL	VALUE
91189	Best Bitter Brls	25.50	100	2550.00
92258	Master Brew Mild Brls	20.00	200	4000.00
9238X	Stock Ale Brls	15.00	100	1500.00
.				.
.				.
			TOTAL	8050.00

4. A text file contains the following three fields per line.

name of a television programme	: STRING[30];
estimated size of viewing audience (millions)	: REAL;
category of programme	: CHAR;

where the third field is coded as follows:

D - drama
L - light entertainment
N - natural history
S - sport

A typical record from the file might contain the following data:

Inspector Morse   12.5 D

and indicates that the television programme Inspector Morse was watched by 12.5 million viewers, and falls in the category of drama.

    a. Using an editor create the text file with programmes of your own choice.

    b. Sort the contents of this file on the category code as the key. This will group all the drama programmes together, all the light entertainment programmes together, etc.

    c. Write a program to input a category code and generate a report on the names of all the programs in that category, together with the audience viewing figures and finally the total number of viewers who watched programmes in that category.

5. Create a text file that contains the following information about a persons transactions for a bank account.

date of transaction	:	STRING[5] in the format ddmmm
description of transaction	:	STRING[20]
credit or debit	:	CHAR
amount of transaction	:	REAL

A typical transaction record might appear in the file as follows:

    18MAR Electricity Company D 32.00

The file is sorted on the date of the transaction, therefore it is important to limit the choice of your dates to only one month. The file should not contain more than, say ten transactions.

Write a program to read the file and print a bank statement similar to the one shown in figure 1.12 in the first chapter. Assume for the purpose of this exercise that the name of the acount, year, sheet number and account number are literals coded in the program and not variables.

6. Create a text file containing one field per line as follows:

    car registration number   : STRING

For example,

    SPR 953
    UTK 902L
    A814KFC
    A344DGU
    H705DUD
    K374 UUD

Create a second text file containing four fields per line as follows:

date of registration of vehicle	: integer YYMM
name of owner	: STRING[20]
address of owner	: STRING[30]
date of expiry of excise licence	: integer YYMM

For example:

6410	H.Tring	20 Melbourne Crt. Poole	9409
7208	M.Evans	16 Cranbrook Rd. Bath	9308
8501	P.Jones	14 High St. Wimborne	9412
8408	S.Spencer	78 Wild Drive, Crewe	9407
9103	P.Blandford	Parkmead Pl, Bucks	9408
9209	B.Brush	18 March Rd, London W1	9408

The order of each line in the first file corresponds to the order of each line in the second file such that the vehicle registration number **SPR 953** in the first file, corresponds to the vehicle details **6410 H.Tring 20 Melbourne Crt. Poole 9409** in the second file.

Write program to:

a. Read the second file and copy each line to a record in a direct access file.

b. Input a car registration number, search the first text data file for the registration number and if found compute the record position that corresponds to this registration number. Use this value as the direct access record key to read the direct access file and display the details relevant to that vehicle.

c. Display a report on all those vehicles whose excise licences have expired.

9.
Miscellany

This final chapter is used to include those aspects of the language that could not be fitted into the previous chapters of the book, yet are important if the reader is to be given a thorough grounding in the fundamentals of Pascal.

9.1 Data types revisited

A programmer is allowed to create new data types. Enumerated types define ordered sets of values by enumerating the identifiers that denote these values. Their ordering follows the sequence in which the identifiers are enumerated. Enumerated types, by definition, must also be ordinal.

The purpose of creating enumerated types is to improve the documentation of a program. It is not necessary to invent arbitrary codes to quantify values, and the associated enumerated values can be used directly in a program. For example, in a program that specifies different newspapers the type newspaper could be declared as:

```
TYPE
    newspaper = (Times,Telegraph,Today,Mail,Express,Sun,Observer);
```

and an associated variable PaperName could be declared as having the type newspaper.

```
VAR
    PaperName : newspaper;
```

Notice from this example that enumerated types are declared using the format:

```
identifier = (list of values)
```

Within a program it would be legal to assign an enumerated value to PaperName:

```
PaperName := Telegraph;
```

Notice that it is not necessary to enclose the enumerated literal with apostrophes since the value is not a string.

Warning! It would be illegal to use Read, ReadLn, Write or WriteLn to input or output values of enumerated type.

Values from one list of an enumerated type cannot be used to form part of another list for a different enumerated type. For example the following declarations would be illegal.

```
TYPE
    DaysOfWeek = (Sun,Mon,Tue,Wed,Thu,Fri,Sat);
    DaysNotWorking = (Sun,Wed,Sat);
```

9.2 Subrange types

Any ordinal data type may be declared in terms of a range of values from within the type. For example if the price of newspapers was to range from 15p to 65p, then a type declaration for price would be:

```
TYPE
    price = 15..65;
```

where price is defined implicitly as being composed of values in the range 15 through to 65 of data type integer. A variable that represents the cost of a newspaper could then be declared as:

```
VAR
    CostOfPaper : price;
```

Subranges can also be declared for enumerated types since their values are ordinal. For example:

```
TYPE
    newspaper = (Times,Telegraph,Today,Mail,Express,Sun,Observer);
    tabloid = Today..Sun;
VAR
    PopularPress : tabloid;
```

Within a program the variable PopularPress can be assigned any of the values Today, Mail, Express or Sun.

A further example of an enumerated type might be:

```
TYPE
    month = (Mar,Apr,May,Jun,Jul,Aug,Sep,Oct,Nov,Dec,Jan,Feb);
```

with a declaration of the following subranges.

```
    Spring=Mar..May;
    Summer=Jun..Aug;
    Autumn=Sep..Nov;
    Winter=Dec..Feb;
VAR
    SummerHoliday : Summer;
    WinterHoliday : Winter;
```

Both variables are of the type month with the subranges specified. The variable WinterHoliday can only be assigned the values Dec, Jan or Feb. Notice that if month had been specified as:

```
month = (Jan,Feb,Mar,Apr,May,Jun,Jul,Aug,Sep,Oct,Nov,Dec);
```

the declaration of the subrange Winter=Dec..Feb would be illegal, since the ordinal value of Dec is greater than the ordinal value for Feb.

9.3 Predefined functions

As early as chapter one, in table 1.2, the reader was introduced to a list of words that must not be used as programmer defined identifiers. Amongst this list was a list of predefined functions that included CHR, EOF, EOLN, and ORD. These four functions have already been introduced in previous chapters. The common feature about them is that they all return a value. For example, CHR returns the value of a type whose ordinal position is specified, CHR(65) = 'A'; ORD returns the position of an ordinal value, ORD('A') = 65; and both EOF and EOLN return either TRUE or FALSE.

Further predefined functions include SUCC and PRED that return the values of the successor and predecessor, respectively, of ordinal types. For example the ASCII character set is an ordinal data type CHAR, therefore, the SUCC('J') is 'K', and the PRED('J') is 'I'.

157

Similarly with the INTEGER type, SUCC(0) is +1, PRED(0) is -1.

Given the declaration

month = (Jan,Feb,Mar,Apr,May,Jun,Jul,Aug,Sep,Oct,Nov,Dec);

PRED(May) is Apr; SUCC(Sep) is Oct; PRED(Jan) and SUCC(Dec) would both return an error, since Jan does not have a predecessor and Dec does not have a succesor in the list.

The following mathematical functions are available in Pascal.

name	description	argument	result
ABS	absolute value of argument	real/integer	same as argument
ARCTAN	the arc tangent of the argument	real/integer	real
COS	the cosine of the argument	real/integer	real
EXP	the value e raised to the power of the argument	real/integer	real
LN	the logarithm to the base e of the argument	real/integer	real
ODD	true if the argument is odd	integer	Boolean
SIN	the sine of the argument	real/integer	real
SQR	the square of the argument	real/integer	same as argument
SQRT	the positive square root of the argument	real/integer	real

The examples that follow represent an interpretation of the meaning of the mathematical functions listed. Note that all angles are represented in radians and not degrees.

ABS(X) returns the absolute value of X. e.g. ABS(-3.7) = 3.7.

ARCTAN(X) returns the arc tangent of X (the angle whose tangent is X) e.g. ATN(1)=0.7854... since the tangent of 45 degrees (0.7854.. radians) = 1.

COS(X) returns the cosine of X e.g. COS(1.0472) = 0.5. Note 60 degrees = 1.0472 radians.

EXP(X) returns the exponent of X e.g EXP(1) = 2.71828. Note e=2.71828...

LN(X) returns the natural logarithm of X where X>0 e.g. LOG(2.71828) = 1; LOG(1)=0.

ODD(X) returns the Boolean value TRUE if X is odd, otherwise returns FALSE if X is even. X must be an integer e.g. ODD(3) is TRUE, ODD(4) is FALSE.

SIN(X) returns the sine of X, e.g. SIN(0.5236)=0.5. Note 30 degrees = 0.5236 radians.

SQR(X) returns the square of the argument e.g. SQR(-10) = 100.

SQRT(X) returns the positive square root of the argument, e.g. SQRT(10)=3.162277...

9.4 Explicit functions

Clearly it is not possible to provide all the functions (mathematical and non-mathematical) that a programmer may require. Incorporated into Pascal is a feature that allows a programmer to define explicitly any function. The syntax of a function definition is almost the same as that of a procedure. However, the name of the function serves as an output parameter in a function, and must therefore be declared as a specific data type. The syntax of a function is given in figure 9.1. The format of the parameter list is identical to that described for a procedure.

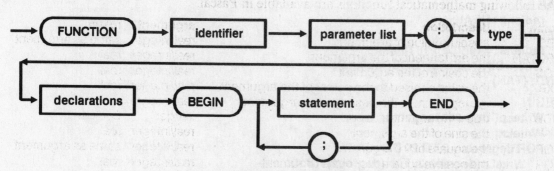

figure 9.1 syntax of a function

As an illustration of the construction of a function consider the following code to define a function for the tangent of an angle. The formal parameter list will consist of an input parameter only. The name of the function is assigned a value within the function body.

```
FUNCTION TAN(angle : INTEGER) : REAL;
{
function that returns the tangent of an angle that is given in degrees
}
CONST
    PI = 3.14159;
VAR
    angle : REAL;
BEGIN
    radians:=(angle * PI)/180;
    TAN := SIN(radians) / COS(radians);
END; {TAN}
```

A function can be tested, using a test harness, in the same manner as a procedure. The position of a function inside a program is the same as that of a procedure. The following program displays the tangents of angles between 0 degrees and 20 degrees in steps of 1 degree. The function is called in exactly the same manner as any other function, i.e. function name followed by argument(s). In this example the function has been called by TAN(degrees). Since a function returns a value, it would be normal to find a function as part of an assignment statement, e.g. tangent := TAN(degrees), where tangent is a variable of type REAL. However, in the following program the function call has been deliberately written in the WriteLn statement to save introducing an extra variable and an assignment statement.

```
PROGRAM TrigTable(OUTPUT);
{
program to print a table of tangents from 0 - 20 degrees
}
VAR
    degrees : INTEGER;

FUNCTION TAN(angle:INTEGER) : REAL;
CONST
PI = 3.14159;
VAR
    radians : REAL;
BEGIN
    radians := (angle*PI)/180;
    TAN:=SIN(radians) / COS(radians);
END; {TAN}

BEGIN
    WriteLn('degrees tangent');
    WriteLn;
    FOR degrees:=0 TO 20 DO
        WriteLn(degrees:2, TAN(degrees):18:4);
    {END FOR}
END. {TrigTable}
```

degrees	tangent
0	0.0000
1	0.0175
2	0.0349
3	0.0524
4	0.0699
5	0.0875
6	0.1051
7	0.1228
8	0.1405
9	0.1584
10	0.1763
11	0.1944
12	0.2126
13	0.2309
14	0.2493
15	0.2679
16	0.2867
17	0.3057
18	0.3249
19	0.3443
20	0.3640

9.5 Sorting

In this section one method of sorting keys held in an array will be explained. Figure 9.2 illustrates the movement of keys in a one- dimensional array, when a selection sort is used to place the keys into ascending order (lowest value to highest value).

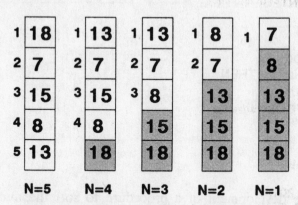

Figure 9.2 An illustration of a selection sort

The contents of the cells from 1 to 5 are inspected for the largest number (18), and when found swapped with the number in cell 5.

The contents of the cells from 1 to 4 are inspected for the largest number (15), and when found swapped with the number in cell 4.

The contents of the cells from 1 to 3 are inspected for the largest number (13), and when found swapped with the number in cell 3.

The contents of the cells from 1 to 2 are inspected for the largest number (8), and when found swapped with the number in cell 2.

When there is only the contents of cell 1 to inspect the numbers are assumed to have been sorted into ascending order.

To generalise, for numbers stored in the cells of an array from 1 to N, the largest number from 1 to N cells is found, and swapped with the number in cell N. The process is repeated, with N being decreased by 1 each time until N=1.

This method of sorting numbers can be developed into a procedure in two parts. The first part is to define a function that will find the position of the largest element in any sized array that is subscripted from 1 to size.

```
FUNCTION PositionOfLargest(size:INTEGER) : INTEGER;
{
function to return the position of the largest integer in the array bounds 1..size
}
VAR
    largest    : INTEGER;
    cell       : INTEGER;
BEGIN
    largest := numbers[1];
    PositionOfLargest := 1;
    FOR cell:= 2 TO size DO
        IF numbers[cell] > largest THEN
        BEGIN
            largest := numbers[cell];
            PositionOfLargest:=cell;
        END; {IF}
    {END FOR}
END; {PositionOfLargest}
```

The second part of the development of a procedure to sort the numbers uses this function embedded within a procedure that passes through the array until all the numbers are sorted.

```
PROCEDURE sort(VAR numbers:table; size:INTEGER);
{
procedure to sort an array of numbers of any size
}
VAR
    index      : INTEGER;
    temp       : INTEGER;
    position   : INTEGER;

    FUNCTION PositionOfLargest(size:INTEGER) : INTEGER;
        .
        .
        .
    END; {PositionOfLargest}
BEGIN
    FOR index:=size DOWNTO 1 DO
    BEGIN
        position:=PositionOfLargest(index);
        temp:=numbers[index];
        numbers[index]:= numbers[position];
        numbers[position]:=temp;
    END; {FOR}
END; {sort}
```

The following program reads a text file containing integers. The number of integers is not known in advance, but must not exceed 100. Displays the numbers that it has stored in an array, then sorts numbers into ascending order using the selection sort, and finally displays the contents of the sorted array.

```
PROGRAM SortDemo(INPUT, OUTPUT);
{
program to demonstrate an algorithm for a selection sort
}
CONST
   N=100;
TYPE
   table = ARRAY[1..N] OF INTEGER;
VAR
   numbers : table;
   size        : INTEGER;

PROCEDURE sort(VAR numbers:table; size:INTEGER);
{
procedure to sort an array of numbers of any size
}
VAR
   index     : INTEGER;
   temp      : INTEGER;
   position  : INTEGER;

   FUNCTION PositionOfLargest(size:INTEGER) : INTEGER;
   {
   function to return the position of the largest integer in the array bounds 1..size
   }
   VAR
      largest : INTEGER;
      cell : INTEGER;
   BEGIN
      largest := numbers[1];
      PositionOfLargest := 1;
      FOR cell:= 2 TO size DO
         IF numbers[cell] > largest THEN
         BEGIN
            largest := numbers[cell];
            PositionOfLargest:=cell;
         END; {IF}
      {END FOR}
   END; {PositionOfLargest}
BEGIN
   FOR index:=size DOWNTO 1 DO
   BEGIN
      position:=PositionOfLargest(index);
      temp:=numbers[index];
      numbers[index]:= numbers[position];
      numbers[position]:=temp;
   END; {FOR}
END; {sort}
```

163

```
PROCEDURE DataInput(VAR numbers : table; VAR size : INTEGER);
{
procedure to input numbers from a test file and store them in an array
}
VAR
   value : INTEGER;
   data : TEXT;
BEGIN
   size:=0;
   ASSIGN(data, 'b:number.txt');
   RESET(data);
   WHILE NOT EOF(data) DO
   BEGIN
      size:=size+1;
      ReadLn(data, numbers[size]);
   END; {WHILE}
   RESET(data);
END; {DataInput}

PROCEDURE DataOut(numbers : table; size : INTEGER);
{
procedure to display an array of any size
}
VAR
   index : INTEGER;
BEGIN
   FOR index:= 1 TO size DO
   BEGIN
      IF index MOD 10 = 0 THEN
         WriteLn;
      {END IF}
      Write(numbers[index]:6);
   END; {FOR}
   WriteLn;
END; {DataOut}

BEGIN
   DataInput(numbers, size);
   DataOut(numbers, size);
   sort(numbers, size);
   DataOut(numbers, size);
END. {SortDemo}
```

```
 56  89   4  67  13 389   5 234 -36
 88  21  30 101
-36   4   5  13  21  30  56  67  88
 89 101 234 389
```

9.6 Searching

The concept of searching for information is not new to the reader. In the chapter 7 there were several examples of searching the contents of an array for information. However, in those examples it was necessary to search through the entire contents of the array to discover that the item was not in the array. Searching an array for data that does not exist in the array is clearly a waste of time. If the information held in the array was sorted into search key order then it would not be necessary to search through an entire array before discovering that the information is not present.

Consider for a moment the following information held in an array in alphabetical order on name as a key. Alphabetically Florence is before John, John is before Michael, Michael is before Penelope, etc. Normally names would be ordered on surname and not forename.

Florence Evans	17 High Court	Witney	OX8 4DF
John Davies	1 Short Drive	Oxford	OX5 3ER
Michael Fielding	80 Baker Street	Bournemouth	BH7 6GH
Penelope Farthing	76 Grange View	Poole	BH15 6GH
Rachel Adams	414 Long Street	London	EC1 7GH
Robert Rankin	23 Sea View	Southampton	SO2 9QT

If a search was to be made on the contents of the array for the key George Davies then the following comparisons would be necessary before it was discovered that George Davies was not in the array.

George Davies is alphabetically greater than Florence Evans so may be found further on in the array. George Davies is alphabetically less than John Davies therefore, an entry for George Davies cannot exist in the array since the names are ordered into alphabetical sequence.

By sorting the contents of the array into alphabetical order on the name of each person only two key comparisons were necessary before discovering that George Davies did not exist in the array. If the array had not been sorted by name then every name in the array would have been compared before it was discovered that the name did not exist in the array.

Assuming that the records are stored into consecutive array locations from 1 through to 6, the following algorithm is used in searching for a name in the array.

A Boolean variable found is initialised to FALSE, and an index used to access each cell of the array is initialised to 1.

While the value of the index is within the limits of the array (1 to 6) and a key match is not found the search for the key continues.

If the key is equal to the name field in the cell being examined, the record is found and the Boolean variable found is set to TRUE. The position in the array of located record, that is the value of the index, is also assigned to a variable called position.

If the key is less than the name field in the cell being examined then the record cannot exist in the array, and the index is set to zero as a means of triggering an exit from the search routine.

If the key is greater than the name field in the cell being examined then the record may exist further down the array, and the value of the index is increased ready to examine the contents of the next cell.

Access to the name field of any record held in the array called contents is through contents[index].name.

```
found:=FALSE;
index:=1;
WHILE (index > 0) AND (index < = size) AND NOT found DO
BEGIN
   IF key = contents[index].name THEN
   BEGIN
      position:=index;
      found:=TRUE;
   END
   ELSE
      IF key < contents[index].name THEN
         index:=0
      ELSE
         index:=index+1;
      {END IF}
   {END IF}
END; {WHILE}
```

In the following program the contents of a text file is read, line by line, into a one-dimensional array. The array is then sorted on the key field name. A user is invited to type the name of a person, and the contents of the array is searched for the name of the same person. If a key match was possible the remaining contents of the record is displayed, otherwise the user is notified that the person's name does not exist in the array.

```
PROGRAM SortAndSearch(INPUT, OUTPUT);
{
program to demonstrate sorting an array of records, then searching for a particular record
}
CONST
   N=50;

TYPE
   entry =  RECORD
               name        : STRING[20];
               street      : STRING[20];
               town        : STRING[15];
               postcode    : STRING[8];
            END;
```

166

```
    table = ARRAY[1..N] OF entry;
VAR
    contents        : table;
    size            : INTEGER;
    key             : STRING;
    found           : BOOLEAN;
    NoMoreData      : BOOLEAN;
    position        : INTEGER;

PROCEDURE sort(VAR contents:table; size:INTEGER);
{
procedure to sort an array of numbers of any size
}
VAR
    index       : INTEGER;
    temp        : entry;
    position    : INTEGER;

    FUNCTION PositionOfLargest(size:INTEGER) : INTEGER;
    {
    function to return the position of the largest integer in the array bounds 1..size
    }
    VAR
        largest : STRING[20];
        cell : INTEGER;
    BEGIN
        largest := contents[1].name;
        PositionOfLargest := 1;
        FOR cell := 2 TO size DO
            IF contents[cell].name > largest THEN
            BEGIN
                largest := contents[cell].name;
                PositionOfLargest := cell;
            END; {IF}
        {END FOR}
    END; {PositionOfLargest}

BEGIN
    FOR index := size DOWNTO 1 DO
    BEGIN
        position := PositionOfLargest(index);
        temp := contents[index];
        contents[index] := contents[position];
        contents[position] := temp;
    END; {FOR}
END; {sort}
```

```
PROCEDURE DataInput(VAR contents : table; VAR size : INTEGER);
{
procedure to transfer contents of text file to array
}
VAR
    data : TEXT;
BEGIN
    size:=0;
    ASSIGN(data, 'B:LIST.TXT');
    RESET(data);
    WHILE NOT EOF(data) DO
    BEGIN
        size:=size+1;
        WITH contents[size] DO
            ReadLn(data, name, street, town, postcode);
    END; {WHILE}
    RESET(data);
END; {DataInput}

PROCEDURE continue(VAR NoMoreData : BOOLEAN);
{
ask whether user wishes to continue
}
VAR
    reply : STRING;
BEGIN
    Write('do you want to continue? - answer yes or no ');
    ReadLn(reply);
    IF reply = 'no' THEN
        NoMoreData:=TRUE
    ELSE
        NoMoreData:=FALSE;
    {END IF}
END; {continue}

PROCEDURE search(    VAR contents : table; size : INTEGER; key : STRING;
                     VAR position:INTEGER; VAR found : BOOLEAN);
{
procedure to search for an item in the array
}
VAR
    index : INTEGER;
BEGIN
    found:=FALSE;
    index:=1;
    WHILE (index 0) AND (index <= size) AND NOT found DO
    BEGIN
        IF key = contents[index].name THEN
        BEGIN
            position:=index;
```

```
            found:=TRUE;
      END
      ELSE
         IF key < contents[index].name THEN
            index:=0
         ELSE
            index:=index+1;
         {END IF}
      {END IF}
   END; {WHILE}
END; {search}


PROCEDURE InputKey(VAR key:STRING);
{
procedure to input a key, left-justify and fill with spaces
}
CONST
   space = ' ';
VAR
   index : INTEGER;
BEGIN
   Write('find? '); ReadLn(key);
   FOR index:=ORD(key[0])+1 TO 20 DO
      key[index]:=space;
   {END FOR}
   key[0]:=CHR(20);
END; {InputKey}


BEGIN
   DataInput(contents, size);
   sort(contents, size);
   REPEAT
      InputKey(key);
      search(contents, size, key, position, found);
      IF found THEN
         WITH contents[position] DO
            WriteLn(street, town, postcode)
      ELSE
         WriteLn(key, ' not listed');
      {END IF}
      continue(NoMoreData);
   UNTIL NoMoreData;
END. {SortAndSearch}
```

```
find? John Davies
1 Short Drive          Oxford     OX5 3ER
do you want to continue? - answer yes or no yes
find? George Davies
George Davies not listed
do you want to continue? - answer yes or no yes
find? Penelope Farthing
76 Grange View         Poole      BH15 6GH
do you want to continue? - answer yes or no no
```

9.7 Summary

● A programmer can create an unlimited number of new data types, known as enumerated types.

● All enumerated types are ordinal, since they are composed from a unique set of objects presented in a predefined order.

● The functions ORD, PRED, SUCC can be applied to objects of enumerated type.

● A programmer can define subrange types from enumerated types, specifying a restriction on the objects that form the new type.

● Pascal provides the programmer with a number of predefined functions that include mathematical functions.

● The language permits the programmer to explicitly define functions.

● All functions have one feature in common, that is they all return a value. For this reason an explicit function must be assigned a data type when it is declared, and the function can either be used in an assignment statement or in Write and WriteLn statements.

● Data that is stored in an array can be sorted into a pre- defined order.

● Provided that a file is not too large, its contents may be read and copied into an array. The contents of the array can then be sorted on a particular key, and the sorted contents written to a new file.

● Searching an array or file of data is made considerably easier if the data has been ordered.

9.8 Questions

1. Declare enumerated data types for:

    a. the operators + - * /;

    b. the four playing-card suits;

    c. the thirteen cards of a playing-card suit;

    d. The four points of a navigational compass.

2. Declare subrange types for:

    a. decimal digits;

    b. a code number that represents the week of a year;

    c. the range of a compass used for navigation;

    d. a three-digit identity code that starts at 100;

    e. the alphabet.

3. Using table 1.1 ASCII codes and characters from chapter one, evaluate the following expressions.

    a. PRED(PRED(PRED('A')));

    b. SUCC(SUCC(SUCC('Z')));

    c. ORD(PRED(SUCC(':')));

    d. SUCC(CHR(80)).

4. If $LOGb(X) = LOGa(X)/LOGa(b)$ thern derive a function to calculate the logarithm of a number of any valid given base. Use this function in writing a computer program to find the logarithms of the numbers from 2 to 10 in steps of 0.5 to the bases 2 to 10 in steps of 2. Your output should be in the form of a table having the numbers down the page and the bases across the page.

5. The median of a set of numbers is that number which has the same number of values above and below it. For example, in the set [0,3,9,18,7,5,4] the median is 5 since three numbers are larger [7,9,18] and three numbers are smaller [0,3,4] than 5. Write a program to compute the median of a set of non-zero integer numbers input to the computer:

a. for an odd number of values;

b. for an even number of values.

Note: clearly for an odd number of values the median will be the central value of the ordered set of numbers. An even number of values will not have one central value, but two central values. The median is taken to be the average of the two central values.

Answers

This section contains the answers to the questions found at the end of each chapter.

Contents

Facts and figures - answers to section 1.9

1.

The data in the 'Used Cars for Sale', figure 1.11, are the details about each car and the price of each car. In Pascal this might be described as:

```
VAR
        details : STRING;
        price   : INTEGER;
```

In declaring the price of the car as being of type INTEGER, it is assumed that there will be no price greater than £32767.

The data in the 'Statement of Account', figure 1.12, will cover such items as the name of the account, the year, the sheet number, the account number, the date of a transaction, the description of the transaction, the amount of the transaction, the balance, and whether the balance is in credit or debt.

```
VAR
        NameOfAccount       : STRING;
        year                : INTEGER;
        sheet               : INTEGER;
        AccountNumber       : STRING;
        date                : STRING;
        transaction         : STRING;
        amount              : REAL;
        balance             : REAL;
        credit_debit        : CHAR;
```

The data in the 'Gas Bill', figure 1.13, will cover such items as the name and address of the consumer, the date of the bill, the date of the meter reading, the present and previous meter readings, the amount of gas supplied, the power consumed, the charge for using the amount of gas, the dates of the billing period, the number of days in that period, the standing charge and the final amount due.

```
VAR
        CustomerName        : STRING;
        address             : STRING;
        town                : STRING;
        postcode            : STRING;
        DateOfBill          : STRING;
        DateOfMeterReading  : STRING;
        PresentReading      : INTEGER;
        estimate            : CHAR;
        PreviousReading     : INTEGER;
        GasSupplied         : REAL;
        PowerConsumed       : INTEGER;
        GasCharge           : REAL;
        PreviousDateDD      : INTEGER;
        PreviousDateMM      : INTEGER;
        PreviousDateYY      : INTEGER;
        CurrentDateDD       : INTEGER;
        CurrentDateMM       : INTEGER;
        CurrentDateYY       : INTEGER;
        days                : INTEGER;
        StandingCharge      : REAL;
        AmountDue           : REAL;
```

Note - whenever a date is required in a calculation it is recommended to store the date as three separate integers that represent DDMMYY.

2.

	Illegal variable names	Reason for illegality
(b)	net-pay	hyphen
(d)	cost of paper	embedded spaces
(e)	ReadLn	Predefined procedure
(f)	?X?Y	question marks
(g)	1856AD	variable must start with a letter

Note: Pascal identifiers are NOT case sensitive, therefore, the identifier ReadLn is the same as READLN.

3.

(a) STRING   (b) REAL   (c) INTEGER   (d) CHAR
(e) cannot be represented as an INTEGER suggest change to REAL (or LONGINT in Turbo Pascal)
(f) REAL   (g) INTEGER   (h) INTEGER   (i) INTEGER
(j) cannot be represented as an INTEGER suggest change to REAL (or LONGINT in Turbo Pascal)
(k) REAL

4.

character	ASCII code
A	65
M	77
*	42
a	97
m	109
/	47
?	63
BEL	7
NUL	0
9	57

5.

(a) -8.74458E+02
(b) 1.23456E-03
(c) 1.23456789E+08

6.

(a) Exponent too large - overflow. Note 3.016E+39 is too large to store.
(b) Accuracy of the number will be lost, however, the approximation can be stored 1.23456789010E+09
(c) Exponent too small - underflow. Note -4.56E-43 is too small to store.

7.

A constant can be represented by any of the following formats.

format	example
+ constant identifier	+vat
constant identifier	pi
- constant identifier	-threshold
+ unsigned number	+0.175
unsigned number	3.14159
- unsigned number	-5000
character	'A'
character string	'ABCDEFG'

2. Processing data - answers to section 2.10

1.

(a)	A	B	C	D
	36	36	36	36

(b)	A	B	C	D
	10	14	29	89

(c)	A	B
	48	50

(d)	X	Y
	19	-13

(e)	X	Y	Z
	18	3	54

(f)	A	B
	12.5	2.0

(g)	A	B	X
	16	3	5

(h)	C	D	Y
	18	5	3

2. (a)

```
PROGRAM C2Q2a(OUTPUT);
BEGIN
        WriteLn('Hello World');
END. {C2Q2a}
```

(b)

```
PROGRAM C2Q2b(INPUT, OUTPUT);
VAR
        message : STRING;
BEGIN
        Write('input message ');
        ReadLn(message);
        WriteLn('My message to the World is ', message);
END. {C2Q2b}
```

3.

```
PROGRAM C2Q3(OUTPUT);
VAR
        A, B            : INTEGER;
        answer          : INTEGER;
BEGIN
        A:=5;
        B:=9;
        answer := A+B;
        WriteLn('sum = ', answer);
        answer := A-B;
        WriteLn('difference = ', answer);
        answer := A*B;
        WriteLn('product = ', answer);
        answer := A DIV B;
```

```
          WriteLn('integer division = ', answer);
          answer := A MOD B;
          WriteLn('remainder after integer division = ', answer);
END. {C2Q3}
```

4.

```
PROGRAM C2Q4(INPUT, OUTPUT);
CONST
          InchConv=2.54;
          StoneConv=6.364;
VAR
          name                          : STRING;
          height, weight                : REAL;
          NewHeight, NewWeight          : REAL;
BEGIN
          Write('input your name => ');
          ReadLn(name);
          Write('input your height in inches => ');
          ReadLn(height);
          Write('input your weight in Stones => ');
          ReadLn(weight);
          NewHeight:=height*InchConv;
          NewWeight:=weight*StoneConv;
          WriteLn('PERSONAL DETAILS');
          WriteLn('NAME: ', name);
          WriteLn('HEIGHT (cm): ',NewHeight:4:1);
          WriteLn('WEIGHT (Kg): ',NewWeight:5:2);
END. {C2Q4}
```

5.

```
PROGRAM C2Q5(INPUT, OUTPUT);
VAR
          Fahrenheit, Centigrade:REAL;
BEGIN
          Write('input temperature in degrees Fahrenheit => ');
          ReadLn(Fahrenheit);
          Centigrade:=(Fahrenheit-32.0)*(5.0/9.0);
          WriteLn('equivalent temperature in degrees Centigrade => ', Centigrade:4:1);
END. {C2Q5}
```

6.

```
PROGRAM C2Q6(INPUT,OUTPUT);
CONST
          border=0.5;
          turf=0.75;
VAR
          length, width, GardenArea, LawnArea, cost:REAL;
BEGIN
          Write('input the length and width of the garden => ');
          ReadLn(length, width);
          GardenArea:=length*width;
          LawnArea:=(length-(2.0*border))*(width-(2.0*border));
          cost:=turf*LawnArea;
          WriteLn('Area of garden ',GardenArea:6:1);
          WriteLn('Area of lawn ',LawnArea:6:1);
          WriteLn('cost of turfing lawn £',cost:7:2);
END. {C2Q6}
```

7.

```
PROGRAM C2Q7(INPUT,OUTPUT);
VAR
        money, twenty, ten, five, one:INTEGER;
BEGIN
        Write('input an amount of money in £ => ');
        ReadLn(money);
        twenty:=money DIV 20; money:=money MOD 20;
        ten:=money DIV 10; money:=money MOD 10;
        five:=money DIV 5; one:=money MOD 5;
        WriteLn('breakdown of notes into denominations');
        WriteLn('£20 notes', twenty:6);
        WriteLn('£10 notes', ten:6);
        WriteLn('£5 notes ', five:6);
        WriteLn('£1 coins ', one:6);
END. {C2Q7}
```

8.

```
PROGRAM C2Q8(INPUT, OUTPUT);
VAR
        length, width, shallow, deep, volume:REAL;
BEGIN
        Write('input length => '); ReadLn(length);
        Write('input width => '); ReadLn(width);
        Write('input depth at shallow end => '); ReadLn(shallow);
        Write('input depth at deep end => '); ReadLn(deep);
        volume:=(length*width)*((shallow+deep)/2.0);
        Write('volume of water required to fill the pool is ',volume:10:1);
        WriteLn(' cubic units');
END. {C2Q8}
```

9.

```
PROGRAM C2Q9(INPUT,OUTPUT);
CONST
        pi=3.14159;
        BaseValue=48; {ASCII character for lower character adjacent to 0}
VAR
        character          : CHAR;
        DecimalNumber      : REAL;
BEGIN
        Write('input character in the range 0..9 => '); ReadLn(character);
        DecimalNumber:=pi*(ORD(character)-BaseValue);
        WriteLn('result of computation is ', DecimalNumber:8:4);
END. {C2Q9}
```

10. (a)

```
PROGRAM C2Q10a(INPUT, OUTPUT);
CONST
        numbers=3;
VAR
        x,y,z   : INTEGER;
        mean    : REAL;
BEGIN
        Write('input three integers separated by spaces e.g. 2 5 7 ');
        WriteLn('then press the RETURN key');
        ReadLn(x,y,z);
        mean:=(x+y+z)/numbers;
        WriteLn('arithmetic mean of integers = ', mean:10:2);
END.{C2Q10a}
```

(b)

```
PROGRAM C2Q10b(INPUT, OUTPUT);
CONST
        pi=3.14159;
VAR
        radius              : INTEGER;
        SurfaceArea, volume : REAL;
BEGIN
        Write('input integer value for the radius of the sphere =>');
        ReadLn(radius);
        SurfaceArea:=4*pi*radius*radius;
        volume:=SurfaceArea*radius/3;
        WriteLn('surface area of sphere =',SurfaceArea:10:2);
        WriteLn('volume of sphere =',volume:10:2);
END.{C2Q10b}
```

(c)

```
PROGRAM C2Q10c(INPUT, OUTPUT);
CONST
        VAT=0.175;
VAR
        item1, item2, item3 : REAL;
        SubTotal, Tax, Total : REAL;
BEGIN
        WriteLn('SALES INVOICE'); WriteLn; WriteLn;
        Write('input cost of item 1 ');ReadLn(item1);
        Write('input cost of item 2 ');ReadLn(item2);
        Write('input cost of item 3 ');ReadLn(item3);
        SubTotal:=item1+item2+item3;
        Tax:=SubTotal*VAT;
        total:=SubTotal+Tax;
        WriteLn('Sub Total ', SubTotal:10:2);
        WriteLn('VAT @ 17.5% ', Tax:10:2);
        WriteLn('Total ', Total:10:2);
END.{C2Q10c}
```

3. Making decisions - answers to section 3.9

1.

(a) FALSE   (b) TRUE   (c) TRUE   (d) FALSE   (e) TRUE   (f) TRUE   (g) TRUE

2.

(a) X=Y   (b) X<>Y   (c) A<=B   (d) Q<=T   (e) X>=Y   (f) (X<=Y) AND (A<>B)
(g) (A>18) AND (H>68) AND (W>75)   (h) G<100) AND (G>50)
(i) (H<50) OR (H>100)

3.

A	B	C	output
16	16	32	y
16	-18	32	x
-2	-4	16	z

4.

```
PROGRAM C3Q4(INPUT, OUTPUT);
VAR
        name   : STRING;
        age    : INTEGER;
        height : INTEGER;
        sex    : STRING;
        male   : BOOLEAN;
BEGIN
        Write('input name of suspect '); ReadLn(name);
        Write('age? '); ReadLn(age);
        Write('height? '); ReadLn(height);
        Write('sex? '); ReadLn(sex);
        IF (sex = 'male') THEN
                male := TRUE
        ELSE
                male := FALSE;
        {END IF}
        IF (age >= 20) AND (age <= 25) AND (height >= 66) AND (height <= 70) AND male THEN
                WriteLn(name, ' is a suspect and should be held for interrogation')
        ELSE
                WriteLn(name, ' is not a suspect and should be released');
        {END IF}
END. {C3Q4}
```

5.

```
PROGRAM C3Q5(INPUT, OUTPUT);
CONST
        FlatRate=8; Rate1=12; Rate2=16;
        Normalhours=35; threshold=60;
VAR
        HoursWorked : INTEGER;
        OvertimePay  : REAL;
BEGIN
        Write('input hours worked => ');
        ReadLn(HoursWorked);
        IF HoursWorked > threshold THEN
                OvertimePay:=(threshold-NormalHours)*Rate1 + (HoursWorked-threshold)*Rate2
        ELSE
                IF HoursWorked > NormalHours THEN
                        OvertimePay:=(HoursWorked-NormalHours)*Rate1
                ELSE
                        OvertimePay:=0;
                {END IF}
        {END IF}
        WriteLn('overtime pay => ', OvertimePay:6:2);
END. {C3Q5}
```

6.

```
PROGRAM C3Q6(INPUT, OUTPUT);
CONST
        Band1=999.0; Band2=9999.0; Band3=99999.0;
        Comm1=0.01; Comm2=0.05; Comm3=0.1;
VAR
        sales, commission:REAL;
BEGIN
        Write('input sales figure => ');
        ReadLn(sales);
        IF (sales > Band2) AND (sales <=Band3) THEN
                commission:=sales*Comm3
```

```
        ELSE
                IF (sales > Band1) AND (Sales <= Band2) THEN
                        commission:=sales*Comm2
                ELSE
                        commission:=sales*Comm1;
                {END IF}
        {END IF}
        WriteLn('commission on sales => ',commission:6:2);
END. {C3Q6}
```

7.

```
PROGRAM C3Q7(INPUT, OUTPUT);

VAR
        reading         : CHAR;
        reply           : CHAR;
BEGIN
        WriteLn('input first letter of barometer reading');
        Write('[S]TORM, [R]AIN, [C]HANGE, [F]AIR, [V]ERY DRY ');
        ReadLn(reading);
        CASE reading OF
        'S' : WriteLn('wear overcoat and hat');
        'R' : WriteLn('wear raincaot and take umbrella');
        'C' :   BEGIN
                        Write('did it rain yesterday? answer [y]es or [n]o ');
                        ReadLn(reply);
                        IF reply = 'y' THEN
                                WriteLn('wear jacket and take umbrella')
                        ELSE
                                WriteLn('wear raincoat and take umbrella');
                        {END IF}
                END;
        'F' : WriteLn('wear jacket and take umbrella');
        'V' : WriteLn('wear jacket')
        ELSE
                WriteLn('DATA ERROR - code for barometer reading incorrect');
        END; {CASE}
END. {C3Q7}
```

8.

```
PROGRAM C3Q8(INPUT,OUTPUT);
CONST
        Spring=5.0;Summer=7.5;Autumn=3.75;Winter=2.5; {seasonal hire fluctuations}
        period=7;
        discount=0.25;
        deposit=50;
VAR
        season          :CHAR;
        days            :INTEGER;
        charge          :REAL;
        error           :BOOLEAN;
BEGIN
        error:=FALSE;
        Write('input season code A-Spring, B-Summer, C-Autumn, D-Winter => ');
        ReadLn(season);
        Write('input number of days hire => ');
        ReadLn(days);
        CASE season OF
        'A':charge:=days*Spring;
        'B':charge:=days*Summer;
```

```
        'C':charge:=days*Autumn;
        'D':charge:=days*Winter;
        ELSE
        BEGIN
                WriteLn('error - wrong seasonal code - use A,B,C or D only');
                WriteLn('re-run program');
                error:=TRUE;
        END
        END; {CASE}
        IF NOT error THEN
        BEGIN
                IF days > period THEN
                        charge:=charge*(1.0-discount);
                {END IF}
                charge:=charge+deposit;
                WriteLn('cost of hiring bicycle is ',charge:10:2);
        END;
        {END IF}
END. {C3Q8}
```

4. Repeating statements - answers to section 4.7

1.

```
PROGRAM C4Q1(OUTPUT);
VAR
        counter : INTEGER;
BEGIN
        counter := 0;
        REPEAT
                WriteLn('HELLO WORLD');
                counter:=counter+1;
        UNTIL counter = 10;
END. {C4Q1}
```

2.

```
PROGRAM C4Q2(INPUT, OUTPUT);
VAR
        counter         : INTEGER;
        times           : INTEGER;
        message         : STRING;
BEGIN
        Write('what is your message? '); ReadLn(message);
        Write('how many times do you want it repeated? '); ReadLn(times);
        counter := 0;
        REPEAT
                WriteLn(message);
                counter:=counter+1;
        UNTIL counter = times;
END. {C4Q2}
```

3.

```
PROGRAM C4Q3(OUTPUT);
VAR
        Fahrenheit, Centigrade:REAL;
BEGIN
        WriteLn(' F           C');
        WriteLn;
        Fahrenheit:=32.0;
        WHILE (Fahrenheit <= 212.0) DO
```

```
        BEGIN
                Centigrade:=(Fahrenheit-32.0)*(5.0/9.0);
                WriteLn(Fahrenheit:10:0, Centigrade:10:0);
                Fahrenheit:=Fahrenheit+10.0;
        END; {WHILE}
END. {C4Q3}
```

4.

```
PROGRAM C4Q4(OUTPUT);
CONST
        conversion = 1.609344;
VAR
        miles           : INTEGER;
        kilometres      : REAL;
BEGIN
        WriteLn('MILES          KILOMETRES');
        WriteLn;
        miles:=1;
        WHILE (miles <= 50) DO
        BEGIN
                IF (miles MOD 20 = 0) THEN
                BEGIN
                        WriteLn;
                        WriteLn('MILES          KILOMETRES');
                        WriteLn;
                END; {IF}
                kilometres := miles * conversion;
                WriteLn(miles:2, kilometres:10:2);
                miles:=miles+1;
        END; {WHILE}
END. {C4Q4}
```

5.

```
PROGRAM C4Q5(OUTPUT);
VAR
        counter         :INTEGER;
        result          :REAL;
BEGIN
{a}     counter:=1;
        REPEAT
                Write(counter:3);
                counter:=counter+2;
        UNTIL counter > 29;
        WriteLn;
{b}     counter:=2;
        REPEAT
                result:=counter*counter;
                Write(result:6:1);
                counter:=counter+2;
        UNTIL counter > 20;
        WriteLn;
{c}     result:=0;
        counter:=1;
        REPEAT
                result:=result+(counter*counter);
                counter:=counter+2;
        UNTIL counter > 13;
        WriteLn('sum of squares => ', result:6:1);
{d}     WriteLn('UPPER CASE'); counter:=65;
        REPEAT
```

```
                Write(CHR(counter)); counter:=counter+1;
        UNTIL counter > 90;
        WriteLn;
        WriteLn('lower case'); counter := 97;
        REPEAT
                write(CHR(counter)); counter:=counter+1;
        UNTIL counter > 122;
        WriteLn;
END. {C4Q5}
```

6.

```
PROGRAM C4Q6(INPUT,OUTPUT);
CONST
        sentinel=0;
VAR
        sum,number,counter :INTEGER;
        mean                :REAL;
BEGIN
        sum:=0; counter:=0;
        REPEAT
                Write('input positive integer => '); ReadLn(number);
                WHILE number < sentinel DO
                BEGIN
                        WriteLn('error - input positive integers only');
                        Write('=> '); ReadLn(number);
                END; {WHILE}
                sum:=sum+number; counter:=counter+1;
        UNTIL number=sentinel;
        IF counter <> 1 THEN
        BEGIN
                mean:=sum/(counter-1);
                WriteLn('arithmetic mean of ',counter-1:2,' positive integers is ',mean:7:1);
        END; {IF}
END.{C4Q6}
```

7.

```
PROGRAM C4Q7(INPUT, OUTPUT);
CONST
        OvertimeRate=12;
        NormalHours=40;
        MaxEmployee=10;
VAR
        HoursWorked, OvertimePay, employee, bill:INTEGER;
BEGIN
        bill:=0; employee := 1;
        REPEAT
                Write('input hours worked for employee ', employee:2,' => ');
                ReadLn(HoursWorked);
                IF HoursWorked > NormalHours THEN
                        OvertimePay:=(HoursWorked-NormalHours)*OvertimeRate
                ELSE
                        OvertimePay:=0;
                {END IF}
                WriteLn('overtime pay due £', OvertimePay:4);
                bill:=bill+OvertimePay;
                employee:=employee+1;
        UNTIL employee > MaxEmployee;
        WriteLn;
        WriteLn('total overtime bill is £', bill:4);
END. {C4Q7}
```

8.

```
PROGRAM C4Q8(INPUT, OUTPUT);
VAR
      NextChar:CHAR;
BEGIN
      WHILE NOT EOLN DO
      BEGIN
            Read(NextChar);
            WriteLn('ASCII code for ',NextChar,' => ',ORD(NextChar));
      END; {WHILE}
      ReadLn;
END. {C4Q8}
```

9.

```
PROGRAM C4Q9(INPUT, OUTPUT);
VAR
      largest         : INTEGER;
      number          : INTEGER;
      counter         : INTEGER;
BEGIN
      Write('number? '); ReadLn(number);
      largest:=number;
      counter:=1;
      WHILE counter <> 10 DO
      BEGIN
            Write('number? '); ReadLn(number);
            IF number > largest THEN
                  largest:=number;
            {END IF}
            counter:=counter+1;
      END; {WHILE}
      WriteLn('largest integer input was ', largest:6);
END. {C4Q9}
```

10.

```
PROGRAM C4Q10(INPUT, OUTPUT);
VAR
      character : CHAR;
BEGIN
      WriteLn('input one line of text');
      {read up to the first (}
      Read(character);
      WHILE character <> '(' DO
            Read(character);
      {END WHILE}
      {read and write characters up to but excluding )}
      Read(character);
      WHILE character <> ')' DO
      BEGIN
            Write(character);
            Read(character);
      END; {WHILE}
END. {C4Q10}
```

5. Building Blocks - answers to section 5.11

1.

(a) The actual parameter list is missing in the procedure call to alpha.
(b) The formal parameter list of procedure beta is missing.
(c) The corresponding variable C, between the actual and formal parameter lists is not consistent. C has been defined as a variable yet it appears as a constant 18.
(d) There is a data type mismatch between the actual and formal parameter lists. X and Y are of type CHAR, yet i, j and k are of type INTEGER. Furthermore, the number of parameters in both lists is not the same.

2.

The value of result after each call to procedure test is FALSE, TRUE, FALSE respectively.

3.

```
PROGRAM C5Q3(INPUT, OUTPUT);
VAR
        radius, diameter, circumference, area:REAL;

PROCEDURE calculate(radius:REAL; VAR diameter, circumference, area:REAL);
CONST
        pi=3.14159;
BEGIN
        diameter:=2*radius;
        circumference:=2*pi*radius;
        area:=pi*radius*radius;
END; {calculate}

BEGIN
        Write('radius? '); ReadLn(radius);
        calculate(radius, diameter, circumference, area);
        WriteLn('diameter ', diameter:10:2);
        WriteLn('circumference ', circumference:10:2);
        WriteLn('area ', area:10:2);
END. {C5Q3}
```

4.

```
PROGRAM C5Q4(INPUT,OUTPUT);
CONST
        bell=CHR(7);
VAR
        character       : CHAR;
        value           : STRING;
        success         : BOOLEAN;

PROCEDURE convert(OctalDigit:CHAR; VAR value:STRING; VAR success:BOOLEAN);
BEGIN
        success:=TRUE;
        CASE OctalDigit OF
        '0':value:='zero';
        '1':value:='one';
        '2':value:='two';
        '3':value:='three';
        '4':value:='four';
        '5':value:='five';
        '6':value:='six';
        '7':value:='seven'
        ELSE
                success:=FALSE;
        END; {CASE}
END; {convert}
```

```
BEGIN
      Write('octal digit? '); ReadLn(character);
      convert(character, value, success);
      IF success THEN
              WriteLn(value)
      ELSE
      BEGIN
              WriteLn('DATA ERROR - input character not in range 0..7');
              Write(bell);
      END; {IF}
END. {C5Q4}
```

5.

```
PROGRAM C5Q5(INPUT, OUTPUT);
VAR
      character : CHAR;
      success : BOOLEAN;

PROCEDURE vowel(letter:CHAR; VAR success:BOOLEAN);
BEGIN
      CASE letter OF
      'a','A','e','E','i','I','o','O','u','U' : success:=TRUE
      ELSE
              success:=FALSE;
      END; {CASE}
END; {vowel}

BEGIN
      Write('character? '); ReadLn(character);
      vowel(character, success);
      IF success THEN
              WriteLn(character, ' is a vowel')
      ELSE
              WriteLn(character, ' is NOT a vowel');
      {END IF}
END. {C5Q5}
```

6.

```
PROGRAM C5Q6(INPUT, OUTPUT);
VAR
      junction         : INTEGER;
      signpost         : STRING;
      error            : BOOLEAN;

PROCEDURE WhereTo(JunctNo : INTEGER; VAR destination : STRING; VAR error : BOOLEAN);
BEGIN
      error := FALSE;
      CASE JunctNo OF
      1: destination:='A2 only';
      2: destination:='A228 Snodland Rochester';
      3: destination:='A229 Maidstone Chatham';
      4: destination:='A278 Gillingham';
      5: destination:='A249 Sittingbourne Sheerness';
      6: destination:='A251 Ashford Faversham';
      7: destination:='A2 Canterbury Dover/ A299 Margate Ramsgate';
      ELSE
              error := TRUE;
      END; {CASE}
END; {WhereTo}
```

```
BEGIN
      REPEAT
              Write('input junction number of the M2 '); ReadLn(junction);
              WhereTo(junction, signpost, error);
              IF NOT error THEN
                      WriteLn(signpost)
              ELSE
                      WriteLn('ERROR - Junction number does not exist');
              {END IF}
      UNTIL error;
END. {C5Q6}
```

6. Larger programs - answers to section 6.9

1.

```
PROGRAM C6Q1 (INPUT, OUTPUT);
VAR
      A,E,I,O,U       : INTEGER;
      character       : CHAR;
      LetterIsVowel   : BOOLEAN;

PROCEDURE initialise(VAR A,E,I,O,U : INTEGER);
BEGIN
      A:=0; E:=0; I:=0; O:=0; U:=0;
END; {initialise}

PROCEDURE vowel(letter:CHAR; VAR success:BOOLEAN);
BEGIN
      CASE letter OF
      'a','A','e','E','i','I','o','O','u','U' : success:=TRUE
      ELSE
              success:=FALSE;
      END; {CASE}
END; {VOWEL}

PROCEDURE frequency(letter:CHAR; VAR A,E,I,O,U : INTEGER);
BEGIN
      CASE letter OF
      'a','A'  : A:=A+1;
      'e','E'  : E:=E+1;
      'i','I'  : I:=I+1;
      'o','O'  : O:=O+1;
      'u','U'  : U:=U+1;
      END; {CASE}
END; {frequency}

PROCEDURE display(A,E,I,O,U:INTEGER);
BEGIN
      WriteLn('vowel frequency');
      WriteLn;
      WriteLn('A', A:15);
      WriteLn('E', E:15);
      WriteLn('I', I:15);
      WriteLn('O', O:15);
      WriteLn('U', U:15);
END; {display}

BEGIN
      initialise(A,E,I,O,U);
      WHILE NOT EOLN DO
      BEGIN
```

```
            Read(character);
            vowel(character, LetterIsVowel);
            IF LetterIsVowel THEN
                    frequency(character,A,E,I,O,U);
            {END IF}
      END; {WHILE}
      display(A,E,I,O,U);
END. {C6Q1}
```

2.

```
PROGRAM C6Q2(INPUT, OUTPUT);
VAR
      A,B,C,D                 : INTEGER;
      counter, ClassSize      : INTEGER;
      dist                    : REAL;

PROCEDURE initialise(VAR categoryA, categoryB, categoryC, categoryD : INTEGER;
                    VAR PupilCounter : INTEGER);
BEGIN
      categoryA:=0;
      categoryB:=0;
      categoryC:=0;
      categoryD:=0;
      PupilCounter:=0;
END; {initialise}

PROCEDURE InputClassSize(VAR size : INTEGER);
BEGIN
      REPEAT
            Write('input size of class ');
            ReadLn(size);
      UNTIL size > 0;
END; {InputClassSize}

PROCEDURE InputDistance(VAR distance : REAL);
BEGIN
      REPEAT
            Write('input distance of pupil from school ');
            ReadLn(distance);
      UNTIL distance > 0.0;
END; {InputDistance}

PROCEDURE analysis(distance : REAL; VAR categoryA, categoryB, categoryC, categoryD : INTEGER);
BEGIN
      IF distance < 1.0 THEN
            categoryA := categoryA + 1
      ELSE IF distance < 5.0 THEN
            categoryB := categoryB + 1
      ELSE IF distance < 10.0 THEN
            categoryC := categoryC + 1
      ELSE
            categoryD := categoryD + 1;
      {END IF}
END; {analysis}

PROCEDURE results(categoryA, categoryB, categoryC, categoryD : INTEGER);
BEGIN
      WriteLn('category pupils');
      WriteLn;
      WriteLn('A ', categoryA:2);
      WriteLn('B ', categoryB:2);
```

```
            WriteLn('C ', categoryC:2);
            WriteLn('D ', categoryD:2);
END; {results}

BEGIN
       initialise(A,B,C,D,counter);
       InputClassSize(ClassSize);
       WHILE counter <> ClassSize DO
       BEGIN
                InputDistance(dist);
                analysis(dist,A,B,C,D);
                counter:=counter+1;
       END; {WHILE}
       results(A,B,C,D);
END. {C6Q2}
```

3.

```
PROGRAM C6Q3(INPUT, OUTPUT);
VAR
       angle          : INTEGER;
       s1, s2, s3, s4 : REAL;
       NoMoreData     : BOOLEAN;
       shape          : STRING;

PROCEDURE InputData(VAR angle : INTEGER; VAR side1, side2, side3, side4 : REAL);
BEGIN
       REPEAT
                Write('input size of one internal angle ');
                ReadLn(angle);
       UNTIL (angle > 0) AND (angle < 180);
       REPEAT
                Write('input lengths of the four sides ');
                ReadLn(side1, side2, side3, side4);
       UNTIL (side1 > 0.0) AND (side2 > 0.0) AND (side3 > 0.0) AND (side4 > 0.0);
END; {InputData}

PROCEDURE AnalyseShape(angle : INTEGER; sideA, sideB, sideC, sideD : REAL; VAR name : STRING);
BEGIN
       IF (sideA = sideB) AND (sideB = sideC) AND (sideC = sideD) THEN
              IF angle = 90 THEN
                     name:='SQUARE'
              ELSE
                     name:='RHOMBUS'
              {END IF}
       ELSE
              IF (sideA = sideC) AND (sideB = sideD) THEN
                     IF angle = 90 THEN
                            name:='RECTANGLE'
                     ELSE
                            name:='PARALLELOGRAM'
                     {END IF}
              ELSE
                     name:='IRREGULAR';
              {END IF}
       {END IF}
END; {AnalyseShape}

PROCEDURE display(name : STRING);
BEGIN
       WriteLn('from the size of the internal angle and the lengths');
       WriteLn('of the four sides the figure would appear to be a ');
       WriteLn;
```

```
        WriteLn('----------> ', name, ' <-------------');   WriteLn;
END; {display}

PROCEDURE MoreData(VAR NoMoreData : BOOLEAN);
VAR
        reply : CHAR;
BEGIN
        Write('continue? - answer [Y]es or [N]o ');
        ReadLn(reply);
        IF (reply = 'N') OR (reply = 'n') THEN
                NoMoreData := TRUE
        ELSE
                NoMoreData := FALSE;
        {END IF}
END; {MoreData}

BEGIN
        REPEAT
                InputData(angle, s1,s2,s3,s4);
                AnalyseShape(angle, s1, s2, s3, s4, shape);
                display(shape);
                MoreData(NoMoreData);
        UNTIL NoMoreData;
END. {C6Q3}
```

4.

```
PROGRAM C6Q4(INPUT,OUTPUT);
CONST
        finish='Y';
VAR
        code            : INTEGER;
        reply           : CHAR;
        CostOfCar       : INTEGER;
        percentage      : REAL;
        PolicyType      : STRING;

PROCEDURE DataIn(VAR code:INTEGER; VAR value:INTEGER);
VAR
        age             :INTEGER;
        foreign         :CHAR;
        accident        :CHAR;
        bit0, bit1, bit2 :INTEGER;
BEGIN
        REPEAT
                Write('input age of driver => '); ReadLn(age);
        UNTIL (age>=17) AND (age <=100);
        IF age >=25 THEN bit0:=0 ELSE bit0:=1; {END IF}
        WriteLn('answer either Y(es) or N(o) to the next two questions');
        REPEAT
                Write('is the car foreign? '); ReadLn(foreign);
        UNTIL (foreign='Y') OR (foreign='N');
        IF foreign = 'N' THEN bit1:=0 ELSE bit1:=2; {END IF}
        REPEAT
                Write('accident in last three years? ');ReadLn(accident);
        UNTIL (accident='Y') OR (accident='N');
        IF accident = 'N' THEN bit2:=0 ELSE bit2:=4; {END IF}
        code:=bit2+bit1+bit0;
        REPEAT
                Write('input insured value of car '); ReadLn(value);
        UNTIL value > 0;
END; {DataIn}
```

```
PROCEDURE analysis(code:INTEGER; VAR policy:STRING; VAR percent:REAL);
BEGIN
      CASE code OF
      0 :     BEGIN policy:='10% comprehensive'; percent:=10; END;
      1 :     BEGIN policy:='10% comprehensive + £50 excess'; percent:=10; END;
      2,4:    BEGIN policy:='15% comprehensive'; percent:=15; END;
      3 :     BEGIN policy:='15% comprehensive + £50 excess'; percent:=15; END;
      5 :     BEGIN policy:='7.5% third party only'; percent:=7.5; END;
      6 :     BEGIN policy:='20% comprehensive'; percent:=20; END;
      7 :     BEGIN policy:='decline to issue policy'; percent:=0;END;
      END;{CASE}
END; {analysis}

PROCEDURE display(policy:STRING; percent:REAL; value:INTEGER);
VAR
      premium : REAL;
BEGIN
      WriteLn('Insurance policy: ', policy);
      WriteLn('Car insured for: £', value:6);
      IF percent > 0.0 THEN
      BEGIN
            premium := value * percent /100.0;
            WriteLn('Premium due: £', premium:6:2);
      END; {IF}
END; {display}

PROCEDURE request(VAR reply:CHAR);
BEGIN
      REPEAT
            Write('do you want to finish? '); ReadLn(reply);
      UNTIL (reply='Y') OR (reply='N');
END; {request}

BEGIN
      REPEAT
            DataIn(code, CostOfCar);
            analysis(code, PolicyType, percentage);
            display(PolicyType, percentage, CostOfCar);
            request(reply);
      UNTIL reply=finish;
END. {C6Q4}
```

5.

```
PROGRAM C6Q5(INPUT,OUTPUT);
CONST
      ErrorFactor=1.0E-6; {required to compensate for machine inaccuracy}
VAR
      length, TotalWaste, waste    :REAL;
      L5, L2, TotalL5, TotalL2     :INTEGER;
      {L5 and L2 are the number of 0.5m and 0.2m strips from one length, TotalL5 and TotalL2 are the total
      number of 0.5m and 0.2m strips}

PROCEDURE initialise;
BEGIN
      TotalL5:=0; TotalL2:=0; TotalWaste:=0;
END; {initialise}

PROCEDURE DataIn(VAR length:REAL);
BEGIN
      REPEAT
            Write('input length of moulding (max 2 dec.pl.) => ');
            ReadLn(length);
```

192

```
        UNTIL length >=0.0;
END; {DataIn}

PROCEDURE calculate(length, size:REAL; VAR pieces:INTEGER; VAR waste:REAL);
BEGIN
        pieces:=0; waste:=0;
        WHILE (length+ErrorFactor)>=size DO
        BEGIN
                length:=length-size;
                pieces:=pieces+1;
        END;
        waste:=length;
END; {calculate}

PROCEDURE Results(L5,L2:INTEGER; waste:REAL);
BEGIN
        WriteLn('0.5m 0.2m waste');
        WriteLn(L5:4,L2:8,waste:9:2);
END; {Results}

BEGIN
        initialise;
        DataIn(length);
        WHILE length > 0 DO
        BEGIN
                calculate(length,0.5,L5,waste);
                TotalL5:=TotalL5+L5;
                calculate(waste,0.2,L2,waste);
                TotalL2:=TotalL2+L2;
                TotalWaste:=TotalWaste+waste;
                Results(L5,L2,waste);
                DataIn(length);
        END; {WHILE}
        WriteLn('totals');
        WriteLn('0.5m ',TotalL5:3,' 0.2m ',TotalL2:3,' waste ',TotalWaste:6:2);
END. {C6Q5}
```

6.

```
PROGRAM C6Q6(INPUT,OUTPUT);
CONST
        SingleAllowance=1200;
        MarriedAllowance=2300;
        ChildAllowance=100;
        Band1=1000; Band2=2000; Band3=4000;
        Rate1=0; Rate2=0.2; Rate3=0.3; Rate4=0.4;
        yes='Y';
VAR
        GrossSalary             :REAL;
        PersonalStatus          :CHAR;
        NumberOfChildren        :INTEGER;
        TaxableIncome           :REAL;
        tax                     :REAL;
        reply                   :CHAR;

PROCEDURE DataIn(VAR GrossSalary:REAL; VAR PersonalStatus:CHAR; VAR NumberOfChildren:INTEGER);
BEGIN
        REPEAT
                Write('input gross salary => '); ReadLn(GrossSalary);
        UNTIL GrossSalary > 0;
        REPEAT
                Write('input personal status (M)arried or (S)ingle => ');
```

193

```
                ReadLn(PersonalStatus);
        UNTIL (PersonalStatus='M') OR (PersonalStatus='S');
        REPEAT
                Write('input number of children => '); ReadLn(NumberOfChildren);
        UNTIL (NumberOfChildren >= 0) AND (NumberOfChildren < 15);
END; {DataIn}

PROCEDURE analysis(GrossSalary:REAL; PersonalStatus:CHAR; NumberOfChildren:INTEGER; VAR tax:REAL);
BEGIN
        IF PersonalStatus='S' THEN
                TaxableIncome:=GrossSalary-SingleAllowance
        ELSE
                TaxableIncome:=GrossSalary-MarriedAllowance;
        {END IFf}
        TaxableIncome:=TaxableIncome-(ChildAllowance*NumberOfChildren);
        IF TaxableIncome <= Band1 THEN
                tax:=Rate1*TaxableIncome
        ELSE IF TaxableIncome <= Band2 THEN
                tax:=Rate2*(TaxableIncome-Band1)+(Band1*Rate1)
        ELSE IF TaxableIncome <= Band3 THEN
                tax:=Rate3*(TaxableIncome-Band2)+Rate2*(Band2-Band1)+(Band1*Rate1)
        ELSE
                tax:=Rate4*(TaxableIncome-Band3)+Rate3*(Band3-Band2)+
                Rate2*(Band2-Band1)+(Band1*Rate1);
        {END IF}
END; {analysis}

PROCEDURE Result(tax:REAL);
BEGIN
        WriteLn('amount of tax to pay £', tax:8:2);
END; {Result}

PROCEDURE Request(VAR reply:CHAR);
BEGIN
        Write('do you want to finish (Y)es or (N)o => ');
        ReadLn(reply);
END; {Request}

BEGIN
        REPEAT
                DataIn(GrossSalary, PersonalStatus, NumberOfChildren);
                analysis(GrossSalary, PersonalStatus, NumberOfChildren, tax);
                Result(tax);
                Request(reply);
        UNTIL reply=yes;
END. {C6Q6}
```

7. Data structures - answers to section 7.8

1.

```
PROGRAM C7Q1(OUTPUT);
VAR
        counter         : INTEGER;
        sum             : INTEGER;
        letter          : CHAR;
BEGIN
        FOR counter := 50 TO 75 DO
                Write(counter:3);
        {END FOR}
        WriteLn;
        FOR counter := 20 DOWNTO 5 DO
```

```
            Write(counter:3);
        {END FOR}
    WriteLn;
    FOR counter := 1 TO 29 DO
            IF counter MOD 2 <> 0 THEN
                Write(counter:3);
            {END IF}
        {END FOR}
    WriteLn;
    FOR counter := 2 TO 20 DO
            IF counter MOD 2 = 0 THEN
                Write(counter*counter:6);
            {END IF}
        {END FOR}
    WriteLn;
    sum:=0;
    FOR counter := 1 TO 13 DO
            IF counter MOD 2 <> 0 THEN
                sum := sum + counter*counter;
            {END IF}
        {END FOR}
    WriteLn('sum of squares of odd integers from 1 to 13 is ', sum:5);
    FOR letter := 'a' TO 'z' DO
            Write(letter);
        {END FOR}
    WriteLn;
    FOR letter := 'Z' DOWNTO 'A' DO
            Write(letter);
        {END FOR}
    WriteLn;
END. {C7Q1}
```

2.

```
PROGRAM C7Q2(OUTPUT);
CONST
        alphabet='ABCDEFGHIJKLMNOPQRSTUVWXYZ';
        MaxColumn=26;
VAR
        AlphaString    :ARRAY[1..MaxColumn] OF CHAR;
        index          :INTEGER;
BEGIN
        AlphaString:=alphabet;
        {(a) display alphabet}
        WriteLn(AlphaString);

        {(b) display first six characters}
        FOR index:=1 TO 6 DO
                Write(AlphaString[index]);
        {END FOR}
        WriteLn;

        {(c) display the last ten characters}
        FOR index:=17 TO 26 DO
                Write(AlphaString[index]);
        {END FOR}
        WriteLn;

        {(d) display the tenth character}
        WriteLn(AlphaString[10]);
END. {C7Q2}
```

Answers

3.

```
PROGRAM C7Q3(INPUT, OUTPUT);
CONST
      MaxColumn=8;
TYPE
      numbers=ARRAY[1..MaxColumn] OF INTEGER;
VAR
      X, Y    :numbers;
      index   :INTEGER;
BEGIN
      WriteLn('input eight integers in ascending order');
      FOR index:=1 TO MaxColumn DO
            Read(X[index]);
      {END FOR}
      {store numbers in array Y in reverse order}
      FOR index:=MaxColumn DOWNTO 1 DO
            Y[MaxColumn-index+1]:=X[index];
      {END FOR}
      {display the contents of array Y}
      WriteLn('numbers in descending order');
      FOR index:=1 TO MaxColumn DO
            Write(Y[index]:5);
      {END FOR}
WriteLn;
END. {C7Q3}
```

4.

```
PROGRAM C7Q4(INPUT, OUTPUT);
TYPE
      entry = RECORD
                        exchange    : STRING;
                        STDcode     : STRING;
               END;
      data = ARRAY[1..10] OF entry;
VAR
      DataArray    : data;
      STDkey       : STRING;
      found        : BOOLEAN;
      SizeOfArray  : INTEGER;
      position     : INTEGER;

PROCEDURE DataInput(VAR DataArray:data; VAR size : INTEGER);
VAR
      reply : CHAR;
BEGIN
      size:=0;
      REPEAT
            size:=size+1;
            Write('input exchange => '); ReadLn(DataArray[size].exchange);
            Write('input STD code => '); ReadLn(DataArray[size].STDcode);
            Write('more data? [y]es or [n]o '); ReadLn(reply);
      UNTIL reply = 'n';
END; {DataInput}

PROCEDURE search(VAR DataArray : data; size : INTEGER; key : STRING;
                        VAR found:BOOLEAN; VAR location:INTEGER);
BEGIN
      location:=1;
      found:=FALSE;
      WHILE (location <= size) AND NOT found DO
            IF key = DataArray[location].STDcode THEN
```

```
                found: = TRUE
        ELSE
                location:=location + 1;
            {END IF}
        {END WHILE}
END; {search}

BEGIN
    DataInput(DataArray, SizeOfArray);
    REPEAT
        Write('input STD code => '); ReadLn(STDkey);
        search(DataArray, SizeOfArray, STDkey, found, position);
        IF found THEN
                WriteLn(DataArray[position].exchange)
        ELSE
                WriteLn('key not found - try again');
        {END IF}
    UNTIL found;
END. {C7Q4}
```

5.

```
PROGRAM C7Q5(INPUT, OUTPUT);
TYPE
    matches = ARRAY[1..58] OF BOOLEAN;
    forecast = ARRAY[1..12] OF INTEGER;
VAR
    score_draws  : matches;
    coupon       : forecast;
    draws        : INTEGER;
    index        : INTEGER;

PROCEDURE initialise_draws(VAR score_draws : matches);
VAR
    index : INTEGER;
BEGIN
    FOR index : = 1 TO 58 DO
            score_draws[index]:=FALSE;
    {END FOR}
    WriteLn('input the score draw results in the range 1..58 - zero to exit ');
    WriteLn;
    Write('? '); ReadLn(index);
    WHILE index <> 0 DO
    BEGIN
            score_draws[index]:=TRUE;
            Write('? '); ReadLn(index);
    END; {WHILE}
    WriteLn;
END; {initialise_draws}

PROCEDURE initialise_coupon(VAR coupon : forecast);
VAR
    index : INTEGER;
BEGIN
    WriteLn('input your forecast for matches resulting in a score-draw only');
    WriteLn('using match numbers from 1..58 inclusive');
    WriteLn;
    FOR index:=1 TO 12 DO
    BEGIN
            Write('selection ', index:3, ' ? ');
            ReadLn(coupon[index]);
    END; {FOR}
```

```
        WriteLn;
END; {initialise_coupon}

BEGIN
        initialise_draws(score_draws);
        initialise_coupon(coupon);
        draws:=0;
        FOR index:=1 TO 12 DO
                IF score_draws[coupon[index]] THEN
                        draws:=draws+1;
                {END IF}
        {END FOR}
        WriteLn('number of draws on your coupon this week are ', draws);
END. {C7Q5}
```

6.

```
PROGRAM C7Q6(INPUT, OUTPUT);
TYPE
        food =          RECORD
                                name : STRING;
                                price : REAL;
                        END;
        food_prices = ARRAY[1..10] OF food;
VAR
        menu    : food_prices;
        cost    : REAL;
        item    : STRING;

PROCEDURE initialise(VAR menu : food_prices);
BEGIN
        menu[1].name:='fruit juice';        menu[1].price:=0.30;
        menu[2].name:='soup';               menu[2].price:=0.50;
        menu[3].name:='cold meat salad';    menu[3].price:=2.50;
        menu[4].name:='sausages (2)';       menu[4].price:=1.00;
        menu[5].name:='bacon & egg';        menu[5].price:=1.00;
        menu[6].name:='cod';                menu[6].price:=1.50;
        menu[7].name:='plaice';             menu[7].price:=2.00;
        menu[8].name:='portion of chips';   menu[8].price:=0.75;
        menu[9].name:='tea';                menu[9].price:=0.25;
        menu[10].name:='coffee';            menu[10].price:=0.35;
END; {initialise}

PROCEDURE part_a(VAR menu : food_prices; food_name : STRING; VAR cost : REAL);
VAR
        index : INTEGER;
        found : BOOLEAN;
BEGIN
        index:=1;
        found:=FALSE;
        WHILE (index <=10) AND NOT found DO
                IF food_name = menu[index].name THEN
                        found := TRUE
                ELSE
                        index:=index+1;
                {END IF}
        {END WHILE}
        IF found THEN
                cost:=menu[index].price
        ELSE
                cost:=0;
        {END IF}
END; {part_a}
```

```
PROCEDURE part_b(VAR menu : food_prices);
VAR
      index : INTEGER;
      money : REAL;
BEGIN
      Write('How much have you got to spend? '); ReadLn(money);
      FOR index:=1 TO 10 DO
            IF menu[index].price <= money THEN
                  WriteLn(menu[index].name);
            {END IF}
      {END FOR}
END; {part_b}

PROCEDURE part_c(VAR menu : food_prices);
CONST
      VATrate = 0.175;
VAR
      starter, main, beverage       : STRING;
      cost, vat, total          : REAL;
BEGIN
      total:=0.0;
      Write('starter?' ); ReadLn(starter);
      Write('main course? '); ReadLn(main);
      Write('beverage? '); ReadLn(beverage);
      WriteLn('G r e a s y  S p o o n  C a f e');
      WriteLn;
      WriteLn(starter);
      part_a(menu, starter, cost);
      total:=total+cost;
      WriteLn(' ', cost:6:2);
      WriteLn(main);
      part_a(menu, main, cost);
      total:=total+cost;
      WriteLn(' ', cost:6:2);
      WriteLn('portion of chips');
      part_a(menu, 'portion of chips', cost);
      total:=total+cost;
      WriteLn(' ', cost:6:2);
      WriteLn(beverage);
      part_a(menu, beverage, cost);
      total:=total+cost;
      WriteLn(' ', cost:6:2);
      WriteLn;
      WriteLn('SUBTOTAL ', total:6:2);
      vat:=VATrate * total;
      WriteLn('VAT ', vat:6:2);
      total:=total+vat;
      WriteLn('TOTAL ', total:6:2);
      WriteLn;
END; {part_c}

BEGIN
      initialise(menu);
      Write('input name of food '); ReadLn(item);
      part_a(menu, item, cost);
      WriteLn('cost of ', item, ' is ', cost:6:2);
      part_b(menu);
      part_c(menu);
END. {C7Q6}
```

Answers

7.

```
PROGRAM C7Q7(INPUT, OUTPUT);
TYPE
        months =       RECORD
                                name : STRING;
                                days : INTEGER;
                        END;
        days_in_months = ARRAY[1..12] OF months;
VAR
        month_array   : days_in_months;
        MM            : INTEGER;
        year          : INTEGER;
        LeapYear      : BOOLEAN;
        day           : INTEGER;

PROCEDURE initialise(VAR dim : days_in_months);
VAR
        MM : INTEGER;
BEGIN
        dim[1].name:='January';
        dim[2].name:='February';
        dim[3].name:='March';
        dim[4].name:='April';
        dim[5].name:='May';
        dim[6].name:='June';
        dim[7].name:='July';
        dim[8].name:='August';
        dim[9].name:='September';
        dim[10].name:='October';
        dim[11].name:='November';
        dim[12].name:='December';
        FOR MM:=1 TO 12 DO
                CASE MM OF
                2            :      dim[MM].days:=28;
                4,6,9,11     :      dim[MM].days:=30;
                ELSE
                                    dim[MM].days:=31;
                END; {CASE}
        {END FOR}
END; {initialise}

PROCEDURE TestYear(year : INTEGER; VAR LeapYear : BOOLEAN);
BEGIN
        IF year MOD 4 = 0 THEN
                LeapYear := TRUE
        ELSE
                LeapYear := FALSE;
        {END IF}
END; {TestYear}

PROCEDURE NewYearsDay(year : INTEGER; VAR day : INTEGER);
VAR
        LeapDays : INTEGER;
BEGIN
        day := year - 1993;
        LeapDays := day DIV 4;
        day := (day + LeapDays + 6) MOD 7; if day=0 then day:=7; end;
END; {NewYearsDay}

PROCEDURE PrintCalendar(year : INTEGER; calendar:days_in_months);
VAR
        MM, DD : INTEGER;
```

200

```
            day : INTEGER;
    BEGIN
        WriteLn(year:15);
        WriteLn;
        NewYearsDay(year, day);
        FOR MM := 1 TO 12 DO
        BEGIN
            WriteLn('                              ', calendar[MM].name);
            WriteLn;
            {adjust spacing for first day of month}
            WriteLn(' SUN MON TUE WED THU FRI SAT');
            FOR DD := 1 TO day-1 DO
                    Write('       ');
            {END FOR}
            FOR DD := 1 TO calendar[MM].days DO
            BEGIN
                Write(DD:4);
                IF day MOD 7 = 0 THEN
                BEGIN
                        WriteLn;
                        day:=1;
                END
                ELSE
                        day:=day+1;
                {END IF}
            END; {FOR}
            WriteLn; WriteLn;
        END;
    END; {PrintCalendar}

    BEGIN
        initialise(month_array);
        WriteLn('input year of calendar ');
        ReadLn(year);
        TestYear(year, LeapYear);
        IF LeapYear THEN month_array[2].days := 29; {END IF}
        NewYearsDay(year, day);
        PrintCalendar(year, month_array);
    END. {C7Q7}
```

8. Files of information - answers to section 8.8

1.

```
PROGRAM C8Q1(INPUT, OUTPUT);
VAR
    word            : STRING[15];
    meaning         : STRING[50];
    dictionary      : TEXT;
BEGIN
    ASSIGN(dictionary, 'B:WORDS.TXT');
    RESET(dictionary);
    WHILE NOT EOF(dictionary) DO
    BEGIN
        Read(dictionary, word);
        ReadLn(dictionary, meaning);
        WriteLn(word, meaning);
    END; {WHILE}
END. {C8Q1}
```

2.

```
PROGRAM C8Q2(data, report);
CONST
        UnitCost = 0.04;
VAR
        data, report    : TEXT;
        name            : STRING[20];
        number          : STRING[20];
        previous, current : INTEGER;
        UnitsUsed       : INTEGER;
        charge          : REAL;
BEGIN
        ASSIGN(data,'B:SUBSCR.TXT');
        ASSIGN(report,'B:SUBREP.TXT');
        RESET(data);
        REWRITE(report);
        WriteLn(report,'                    TELEPHONE SUBSCRIBERS');
        WriteLn(report);
        WriteLn(report,'NAME        NUMBER          UNITS       CHARGE');
        WriteLn(report,'                                        USED        £');
        WriteLn(report);
        WHILE NOT EOF(data) DO
        BEGIN
                ReadLn(data, name, number, previous, current);
                UnitsUsed := current - previous;
                charge := UnitCost * UnitsUsed;
                WriteLn(report, name, number, UnitsUsed:5, charge:10:2);
        END; {WHILE}
        RESET(report);
END. {C8Q2}
```

3.

```
PROGRAM C8Q3(data, report);
VAR
        StockNumber : STRING[5];
        description     : STRING[25];
        quantity        : INTEGER;
        price           : REAL;
        data, report    : TEXT;
        value, TotalValue : REAL;
BEGIN
        ASSIGN(data,'b:STOCK.TXT');
        ASSIGN(report,'b:STKREP.TXT');
        RESET(data); REWRITE(report);
        WriteLn(report,'                        STOCK REPORT');    WriteLn(report);
        WriteLn(report,'STOCK       DESCRIPTION              UNIT   LEVEL VALUE');
        WriteLn(report,'NUMBER                               COST');
        WriteLn(report);
        TotalValue:=0;
        WHILE NOT EOF(data) DO
        BEGIN
                ReadLn(data, StockNumber, description, quantity, price);
                value:=price*quantity;
                TotalValue:=TotalValue+value;
                WriteLn(report, StockNumber,' ',description,' ', price:5:2, quantity:8, value:8:2);
        END;{WHILE}
        WriteLn(report);
        WriteLn(report,' TOTAL VALUE ',TotalValue:10:2);
        RESET(report);
END. {C8Q3}
```

4.

```
PROGRAM C8Q4(INPUT, OUTPUT);
VAR
        viewers         : TEXT;
        total           : REAL;
        category        : CHAR;
        programme       : STRING[30];
        audience        : REAL;
        choice          : CHAR;
        exit            : BOOLEAN;
BEGIN
        ASSIGN(viewers, 'B:TV2.TXT');
        RESET(viewers);
        total:=0;
        exit := FALSE;
        Write('input category D, L, N or S '); ReadLn(choice);
        CASE choice OF
        'D' : WriteLn('DRAMA');
        'L' : WriteLn('LIGHT ENTERTAINMENT');
        'N' : WriteLn('NATRURAL HISTORY');
        'S' : WriteLn('SPORT');
        END; {CASE}
        WHILE (NOT EOF(viewers)) AND (NOT exit) DO
        BEGIN
                ReadLn(viewers, category, programme, audience);
                IF choice = category THEN
                BEGIN
                        total:=total+audience;
                        WriteLn(programme, audience:8:2);
                END
                ELSE IF choice < category THEN
                        exit := TRUE;
                {END IF}
        END; {WHILE}
        WriteLn;
        WriteLn('total audience viewing figure ', total:8:2);
END. {C8Q4}
```

5.

```
PROGRAM C8Q5(INPUT, OUTPUT);
VAR
        date : STRING[5];
        transaction : STRING[30];
        c_d : CHAR;
        amount : REAL;
        account : TEXT;
        report : TEXT;
        balance : REAL;
BEGIN
        ASSIGN(account, 'b:bank.txt');
        RESET(account);
        ASSIGN(report, 'b:statemnt.txt');
        REWRITE(report);
        WriteLn(report, '                                        XYZ Bank plc');
        WriteLn(report, 'Mr A.N.Other                            Market Place, Anytown, B1 6PT');
        WriteLn(report);
        WriteLn(report, '                                        Statement of Account');
        WriteLn(report); WriteLn(report);
        WriteLn(report, '1993 sheet 90 Account No.5678910    DEBIT       CREDIT       BALANCE');
        WriteLn(report, '                                        Credit C Debit D');
```

```
        WriteLn(report); WriteLn(report);
        balance:=0.0;
        WHILE NOT EOF(account) DO
        BEGIN
                ReadLn(account, date, transaction, c_d, amount);
                Write(report, date, ' ',transaction);
                IF c_d = 'C' THEN
                BEGIN
                        Write(report, ' ', amount:7:2, ' ');
                        balance:=balance + amount;
                END
                ELSE
                BEGIN
                        Write(report, amount:7:2, ' ');
                        balance:=balance - amount;
                END; {IF}
                Write(report, balance:7:2);
                IF balance > = 0 THEN
                        WriteLn(report, ' C')
                ELSE
                        WriteLn(report, ' D');
                {END IF}
        END; {WHILE}
        Write(report, date, ' BALANCE CARRIED FORWARD ', balance:7:2);
        IF balance > = 0 THEN
                WriteLn(report, ' C')
        ELSE
                WriteLn(report, ' D');
        {END IF}
        RESET(report);
END. {C8Q5}
```

6.

```
PROGRAM C8Q6_a(INPUT, OUTPUT);
TYPE
        information = RECORD
                                date            : INTEGER;
                                name            : STRING[20];
                                address         : STRING[30];
                                expiry          : INTEGER;
                        END;
        registration = FILE OF information;
VAR
        vehicle : registration;
        vehicle_item    : information;
        RecordNo        : INTEGER;
        data            : TEXT;
        DirectAccess    : registration;
BEGIN
        ASSIGN(data, 'B:OWNERS.TXT');
        RESET(data);
        ASSIGN(DirectAccess, 'B:DIRECT.DAF');
        REWRITE(DirectAccess);
        RecordNo:=1;
        WHILE NOT EOF(data) DO
        BEGIN
                WITH vehicle_item DO
                ReadLn(data, date, name, address, expiry);
                SEEK(DirectAccess, RecordNo);
                Write(DirectAccess, vehicle_item);
                RecordNo:=RecordNo+1;
```

```
        END; {WHILE}
        RESET(DirectAccess);
END. {C8Q6_a}

PROGRAM C8Q6_b(INPUT, OUTPUT);
TYPE
        information = RECORD
                                date            : INTEGER;
                                name            : STRING[20];
                                address         : STRING[30];
                                expiry          : INTEGER;
                        END;
        registration = FILE OF information;
VAR
        vehicle_item    : information;
        RecordNo        : INTEGER;
        regno           : TEXT;
        DirectAccess    : registration;
        number          : STRING;
        plate           : STRING;
        reply           : CHAR;
        exit            : BOOLEAN;
BEGIN
        ASSIGN(regno, 'B:REGNO.TXT');
        ASSIGN(DirectAccess, 'B:DIRECT.DAF');
        RESET(DirectAccess);
        REPEAT
                exit := FALSE;
                RecordNo := 0;
                RESET(regno);
                Write('input vehicle registration number '); ReadLn(number);
                WHILE NOT EOF(regno) AND (NOT exit) DO
                BEGIN
                        ReadLn(regno, plate);
                        RecordNo := RecordNo + 1;
                        IF number = plate THEN
                        BEGIN
                                SEEK(DirectAccess, RecordNo);
                                IF NOT EOF(DirectAccess) THEN Read(DirectAccess, vehicle_item); {END IF}
                                WITH vehicle_item DO
                                BEGIN
                                        WriteLn('date ', date:4);
                                        WriteLn('name ', name);
                                        WriteLn('address ', address);
                                        WriteLn('expiry ', expiry:4);
                                        exit := TRUE;
                                END; {WITH}
                        END; {IF}
                END; {WHILE}
        Write('more data? answer [Y]es or [N]o '); ReadLn(reply);
        UNTIL (reply = 'N') OR (reply = 'n');
END. {C8Q8_b}

PROGRAM C8Q6_c(INPUT, OUTPUT);
TYPE
        information = RECORD
                                date            : INTEGER;
                                name            : STRING[20];
                                address         : STRING[30];
                                expiry          : INTEGER;
                        END;
        registration = FILE OF information;
```

```
VAR
        vehicle_item   : information;
        RecordNo       : INTEGER;
        DirectAccess   : registration;
        number         : STRING[7];
        plate          : STRING[7];
        current: INTEGER;
BEGIN
        ASSIGN(DirectAccess, 'B:DIRECT.DAF');
        RESET(DirectAccess);
        Write('input current month and year in format YYMM '); ReadLn(current);
        RecordNo:=1;
        WHILE RecordNo <= FILESIZE(DirectAccess)-1 DO
        BEGIN
                SEEK(DirectAccess, RecordNo);
                IF NOT EOF(DirectAccess) THEN Read(DirectAccess, vehicle_item); {END IF}
                WITH vehicle_item DO
                BEGIN
                        IF expiry < current THEN
                        BEGIN
                                WriteLn;
                                WriteLn('name ', name);
                                WriteLn('address ', address);
                                WriteLn('expiry MMYY', expiry mod 100:3,' ', expiry div 100:2);
                        END;
                END; {WITH}
                RecordNo:=RecordNo+1;
        END; {WHILE}
END. {C8Q6_c}
```

9. Miscellany - answers to section 9.8

1.

a. operator = (+,-,*,/);
b. CardSuits = (clubs, diamonds, hearts, spades);
c. CardValue = (deuce, three, four, five, six, seven, eight, nine, ten, Jack, Queen, King, Ace);
d. points = (North, South, East, West);

2.

a. DecimalDigit = 0..9;
b. week = 1..52;
c. compass = 1..360;
d. IdCode = 100..999;
e. alphabet = 'A'..'Z';

3.

a. >
b.]
c. 58
d. Q

4.

```
PROGRAM C9Q4(OUTPUT);
VAR
        number         :REAL;
        base, Y        :INTEGER; {Y is a FOR loop counter}
```

```
FUNCTION logarithm(base:INTEGER; X:REAL):REAL;
BEGIN
      logarithm:=LN(X)/LN(base);
END; {logarithm}

BEGIN
      WriteLn('NUMBER BASES');
      WriteLn('    2      4      6      8      10');
      number:=2;
      WHILE number <= 10 DO
      BEGIN
            Write(number:4:1);
            FOR Y:=1 TO 5 DO
            BEGIN
                  base:=2*Y;
                  Write(logarithm(base, number):10:4);
            END;
            WriteLn;
            number:=number+0.5;
      END; {WHILE}
END. {C9Q4}
```

5.

```
PROGRAM C9Q5(INPUT, OUTPUT);
CONST
      MaxNumber=40; {cater for a maximum of 40 numbers in the set}
TYPE
      data=ARRAY[1..MaxNumber] OF INTEGER;
VAR
      table                :data;
      NumbersStored        :INTEGER;

PROCEDURE DataIn(VAR NumbersStored:INTEGER);
VAR
      index, datum:INTEGER;
BEGIN
      WriteLn('input a set of numbers - one per line - terminate with 0');
      WriteLn;
      index:=0;
      ReadLn(datum);
      WHILE datum <> 0 DO
      BEGIN
            index:=index+1;
            table[index]:=datum;
            ReadLn(datum);
      END; {WHILE}
      NumbersStored:=index;
END; {DataIn}

FUNCTION median(NumbersStored:INTEGER):REAL;
VAR
      MidPoint:INTEGER;
BEGIN
      MidPoint:=(NumbersStored+1) DIV 2;
      IF ODD(NumbersStored) THEN
            median:=table[MidPoint]
      ELSE
            median:=(table[MidPoint]+table[MidPoint+1])/2.0;
      {END IF}
END; {median}
```

```
PROCEDURE sort(VAR numbers:data; size:INTEGER);
VAR
      index          : INTEGER;
      temp           : INTEGER;
      position       : INTEGER;

      FUNCTION PositionOfLargest(size : INTEGER) : INTEGER;
      VAR
            largest : INTEGER;
            cell : INTEGER;
      BEGIN
            largest:=numbers[1];
            PositionOfLargest:=1;
            FOR cell:=2 TO size DO
                  IF numbers[cell] > largest THEN
                  BEGIN
                        largest:=numbers[cell];
                        PositionOfLargest:=cell;
                  END; {IF}
            {END FOR}
      END; {PositionOfLargest}

BEGIN
      FOR index:=size DOWNTO 1 DO
      BEGIN
            position:=PositionOfLargest(index);
            temp:=numbers[index];
            numbers[index]:=numbers[position];
            numbers[position]:=temp;
      END; {FOR}
END; {sort}

BEGIN
      DataIn(NumbersStored);
      sort(table, NumbersStored);
      IF NumbersStored > 0 THEN
            WriteLn('median of the set of numbers is ', median(NumbersStored):5:1);
      {END IF}
END. {C9Q5}
```

Index